FOLLOW THE WHITE BLAZES

from Georgia to Maine
----
by Pam and John Carr

British hikers' views of the
Appalachian Trail

Published in Great Britain by
Appalachian Walks UK
62 Swarthdale, Haxby,
York YO3 3NZ

Copyright © 1993 Pam & John Carr

ISBN0 9521470 0 9

All rights reserved. No part of this publication may be reproduced or transmitted in any form or by any means, electronic or mechanical, including photocopy, recording, or any information storage and retrieval system without permission in writing from the publishers.

Acknowledgements

In the United States:-

Our thanks to Chuck Young for all the advice and support he gave us, and to his family for making us so welcome in their home.

Also to Jean Cashin and the ATC staff for being there when needed, and to all the volunteers for keeping the Trail so well maintained.

To Jon, Diane, L Jon and Colleen Erdossy for putting up with us; and to Tim and Margaret Ellis, Joan Mackie and Fred Locke for their friendship, moral support and for easing us back into the real world at the end of our adventure.

To all the friendly, generous people we met along the Trail - thanks to you all.

In Britain:-

Special thanks to Joe and Audrey Stephenson at High Paradise Farm for their encouragement and copious pots of tea during our training hikes.

To our son, Andrew, for paying the bills and taking care of our affairs during our absences.

And to Chris Mossop for producing the cover illustration.

Contents

Introduction 7

Chapter 1
    WHAT IS THE APPALACHIAN TRAIL? 9

Chapter 2
    PLANNING OUR HIKE 11

Chapter 3
    CHOOSING EQUIPMENT 13

Chapter 4
    FINAL PLANS 15

Chapter 5
    LIFE ON THE TRAIL 17

Chapter 6
    OUR PROGRESS ALONG THE TRAIL : 1990 21
    Maryland and Pennsylvania : 28 March - 19 April. 21
    Georgia : 26 April - 2 May. 30
    Tennessee and North Carolina : 2 May - 1 June. 34
    Virginia and West Virginia : 1 June - 10 July. 48

Chapter 7
    AFTER THE TRAIL : 1990/1991 66

Chapter 8
    BACK ON THE TRAIL : 1992 67
    Virginia : 1 April - 20 April. 67
    New Jersey and New York : 29 April - 13 May. 76
    Connecticut and Massachusetts : 13 May - 25 May. . . . 87
    Vermont : 25 May - 8 June. 95
    New Hampshire : 9 June - 25 June. 104
    Maine : 25 June - 21 July. 112

Chapter 9
    EQUIPMENT REPORT 137
    Rucksacks. 137
    Tent. 138
    Sleeping-bags. 138
    Cooking Kit 139
    Water Treatment. 139
    First Aid Kit. 140
    Boots. 140
    Clothing. 141
    Camera. 142
    Radio. 143
    Miscellaneous Items. 143

Chapter 10
    FOOD 144

Chapter 11
    FURTHER INFORMATION FOR BRITISH HIKERS . . 147
    U.S. Visas. 147
    Money. 147
    Travel Insurance. 147

The Appalachian Trail

Introduction

We were on holiday in America, driving south on the Blue Ridge Parkway and admiring the beautiful scenery. From time to time we would stop at a viewpoint to stretch our legs and take a longer look at the wooded ridges and valleys of the Appalachian Mountains. At one of these stops we were attracted to a notice-board showing a picture of two hikers with big rucksacks, superimposed on a map of the eastern U S. The message printed above the map read:-

The Appalachian Trail
2,000 miles from Maine to Georgia

One of the longest continuous footpaths in the
world crosses here. The Appalachian Trail winds
through the varied and often remote landscapes of
14 states. In the Great Smokies the trail follows
some of the highest ridges in the Appalachians,
paralleling the Tennessee/North Carolina boundary.

This was in 1985 at Newfound Gap in the Great Smoky Mountains. We were not hikers and we had never before heard of the Appalachian Trail. We were so amazed at the thought of anybody even considering hiking over 2,000 miles, that we photographed the sign to show to equally awestruck friends at home.

On 13th May, 1990 we were back at that sign, having our photograph taken with big rucksacks on our backs - on our way north hiking the 2,146 miles of the Appalachian Trail!

Our life had taken quite a dramatic change in those 4 years. In

1986 we rented a cottage for a holiday in the Lake District and our daughter insisted that we do some fell-walking rather than viewing the scenery from the car. So we were persuaded to buy some sturdy shoes and small rucksacks. Our first expedition was up Skiddaw on the "tourist path", every step was agony and we had to stop for breath every few yards. But when we saw the view from the top we were "hooked" and knew that we must get ourselves fit so that we could spend more time exploring the mountains. As John had taken early retirement, we had time to spend on our new interest so we gradually gained in fitness and experience.

By 1988 we had been enjoying regular day-hikes, when a friend suggested something more challenging - a long-distance walk. Jokingly, John said "Why not the Appalachian Trail?" This sowed the seed in our minds, and before long we were actually planning to do just that. As we had never before camped or carried more than 10lbs on our backs we had to do a lot of training and also research details of the Trail. So we gave ourselves two years to prepare for our big adventure and aimed to set off on 1st April 1990.

Our first problem was to find out about the Trail. We tried libraries and bookshops, but could find no mention of books or maps on the subject. Fortunately a short article appeared in a magazine and the address of the Appalachian Trail Conference (ATC) was given, so we wrote to them at Harpers Ferry in West Virginia. In response to our enquiry we received all sorts of useful information and a book-list, from which we were able to order maps, guide-books and other interesting books to help us plan our trip.

Chapter 1

WHAT IS THE APPALACHIAN TRAIL?

The Appalachian Trail was the brainchild of Benton MacKaye, a regional planner from Massachusetts, who in 1921 proposed a footpath to stretch the length of the Appalachians, to provide an escape to the fresh air of the mountains for thousands of city-dwellers who lived along the east coast of the United States. His idea was for a trail to be built, waymarked and maintained by local volunteer groups, linking together several of the hiking trails which already existed in some areas in the northern states, and building a new trail and forming new hiking clubs in the south. The idea quickly gained support and MacKaye's vision was soon becoming a reality, largely thanks to the enthusiasm of retired judge Arthur Perkins from Connecticut and the efforts and organising ability of lawyer, Myron Avery. At this time there were already hiking clubs in various areas along the proposed route and these were gradually brought together to form the Appalachian Trail Conference.

The ATC co-ordinated the work of the volunteers in choosing the route and building the Trail, and they were soon joined in their efforts by the U.S. Forest Service, National Park Service and crews from the Civilian Conservation Corps. In August 1937 the world's longest continuously waymarked footpath was completed, less than 16 years after the concept was first published. Work then continued on building shelters along the trail, and volunteers still work at maintaining the AT, relocating it where necessary, writing and re-writing guide-books, etc. And the ATC remains a non-profit making organisation, managing and protecting the Trail and adjacent land and co-ordinating the maintenance of the Trail.

Over the years civilisation has crept ever closer to the narrow tract of land that is the AT and has threatened to encroach on the wilderness experience which was MacKaye's dream. Way back in 1937 a plan was proposed to create an "Appalachian Trailway" which would protect land from development on either side of the Trail. This plan worked on land belonging to the U.S. Forest Service and National Park Service but after World War II housing and road building on privately owned land forced 200 miles of the Trail on to roads, so work began to relocate the Trail away from such construction in order to maintain its wilderness character.

In 1968 Congress authorised the Appalachian Trail to become the first "national scenic trail", this gave it official protection and enabled funds to be spent to purchase buffer lands. Ten years later an amendment was passed authorising the purchase of land to create a corridor 1,000' wide, thereby preventing development encroaching on the Trail. By Spring 1993 this project was almost complete with less than 50 miles still unprotected.

The ATC and its clubs now formally have responsibility for maintaining the entire footpath and managing the protected corridor lands, as well as publishing guidebooks, maps and handbooks on trail construction and maintenance. The volunteer Board of Managers and professional staff of 30 at ATC Headquarters, Harpers Ferry, West Virginia, and four small offices along the Trail, co-ordinate all this work, as well as publishing the magazine, "Appalachian Trailway News"; and, with the help of volunteer office staff, answer letters and enquiries from interested hikers from around the world.

Chapter 2

PLANNING OUR HIKE

Once we had learned about the Appalachian Trail we felt even more committed to attempting a "thru-hike". The first thing to decide was whether to go north to south or south to north. Although the official definition states that the AT is a footpath stretching along the ridge of the Appalachian Mountains from Maine to Georgia, we discovered that most thru-hikers travel in the opposite direction, from Georgia to Maine. As spring comes early in Georgia, and very late in Maine, it is best to set out from Springer Mountain in April and hike northwards "with the spring", to arrive at Mount Katahdin in September or early October before the onset of winter. This means that you can enjoy the beautiful spring flowers in the south and the wonderful colours of New England in the autumn. This is what we planned to do, but several hikers each year travel in the opposite direction to avoid the crowds caused by the majority of hikers setting out from Springer Mountain in April.

The Appalachian Trail Conference publishes excellent guide books and maps for the entire Trail, but we obviously didn't want to carry them all for the whole distance. Initially we ordered the book and maps for Georgia so that we could study them at home to get used to the way they are written and laid out. We then bought the subsequent sets as we proceeded along the Trail, either from local stores or hostels if they were available, or by telephone order from ATC who mailed them ahead to a post office of our choosing.

We carried two other ATC publications on our hike, the AT Data Book and the Thru-Hiker's Handbook. These are kept up to date by being republished annually. The Data Book consists of single line entries listing mileages between places on the Trail (e.g. towns, shelters, mountains, road crossings); and also distance and direction to facilities within a short distance off the trail.

The Thru-Hiker's Handbook is written by Dan "Wingfoot" Bruce who has himself thru'-hiked the AT six times. It is full of hints and recommendations on towns and the services available within easy walking distance of the Trail, descriptions and comments on shelters and campsites, water sources, places of interest, viewpoints, historical sites, nature notes, etc. It is like taking an experienced hiker along with you to give a commentary along the way! The Handbook also contains a very good section on planning a thru'-hike, and on how to travel to and from either end of the AT (these pages can be discarded before starting the hike to save weight!)

Chapter 3

CHOOSING EQUIPMENT

At the same time as we were researching the Trail we also started reading walking/camping magazines and scouring outdoor shops to learn about the type of equipment we would need. We knew from our day-hikes that there are some essentials that all hikers should carry - waterproofs, extra clothing, food, water, first-aid kit, compass, maps, torch, etc. But to walk day after day we would also need sleeping-bags, mats, stove and fuel, washing kit............

And, although there are shelters on the Trail, we would need a tent in case we had to spend the night between shelters, or if a shelter was full when we arrived. And big rucksacks to carry all this gear in!

Having read the magazines and picked the brains of any experienced hikers we met when out walking we set out to make our purchases based on their recommendations. As we gradually built up our stock of equipment we soon realised that weight and bulk would be our biggest problems. Over the two years of preparation we made some mistakes; some of the equipment turned out to be too heavy, too bulky or just unsuitable or unnecessary. Our son and daughter were grateful recipients of our rejects!

We were amazed at how "high-tech" backpacking gear has become. No more heavy canvas tents, woollen sweaters and sweaty waterproofs. We were confronted by a bewildering array of strong, lightweight nylon tents (in a variety of strange shapes - tunnels, domes, transverse ridges); polyester pile and fleece jackets; polycotton trousers; wicking underwear; breathable waterproofs. Our minds boggled. Our bank account took a battering!

We had purchased large rucksacks and soon found that they were not large enough. But eventually we had all our gear assembled and packed in new extra-large rucksacks. On the trail our packs weighed between 40 and 50 lbs, varying with the amount of food required between supply points.

Over the 2 year training period we gradually increased both the length of our day-hikes and the weight on our backs. We also practised with our tent, and in July 1989 we hiked the Coast to Coast Walk from west to east. We thoroughly enjoyed our first long hike, although we felt very tired at the end - we had learned that we needed to take a day's rest occasionally and not plod on day after day.

After this walk we also "fine-tuned" our equipment to cut down on weight and bulk. We replaced our synthetic sleeping-bags with down ones, bought a lighter weight stove and threw out several items which had seemed essential, but which we had never used. In September we hiked the West Highland Way and were happy with our gear, so from then on we just kept ourselves in trim by hiking 15 miles a day, 2 or 3 times a week until it was time to leave for America.

Chapter 4

FINAL PLANS

We had arranged for Chuck Young, a member of the ATC, to look after our spare equipment (extra boots, etc) during our hike and also to be our contact should our family need to get in touch with us. As he lives between Washington, DC and Harpers Ferry we decided to fly to Washington so that we could meet him and also visit ATC headquarters before setting foot on the Trail. This gave us the opportunity to pick up all sorts of tips from people who really know the Appalachian Trail.

One recommendation was that it would not be advisable to start out from Springer Mountain in Georgia until mid-April as heavy snows are often experienced in the high southern mountains early in the month. As we had aimed to start on 1st April we did not want to wait around for 2 weeks, so we decided to start hiking north from Harpers Ferry through Maryland and Pennsylvania where the mountain ridges are lower (1500-2000 feet) and then travel south to Georgia.

Entering the 100-mile wilderness
Katahdin from Daicey Pond

Chapter 5

LIFE ON THE TRAIL

Life on the Appalachian Trail is simple, we soon slipped into a routine. Sleeping in the rustic trailside shelters, or our tent, we found that sleep came easily after a day's hike; despite the strange sounds in the woods, the rustling of mice in the shelter or the pattering of rain on the roof. We awoke early as the first light appeared in the sky and the birds began the dawn chorus. It was good to be up early. John would light up the stove and make the tea - a necessary 'jump-start' to get Pam out of her cosy sleeping-bag. Once up we would have a simple breakfast of hot instant oats and tea in cold weather, and orange juice and muesli or poptarts in summer.

After washing the pots and ourselves we packed our kit and were often on our way in little more than an hour of awakening. Especially in the summer this was the best time to walk, before the heat of the day. We were usually the first away from a shelter, which meant that we were clearing the spider webs from across the trail! We frequently set off wearing our lightweight Goretex suits as the trees and undergrowth were often wet with dew or overnight rain.

After about two hours on the Trail we would feel in need of an energy boost, usually a Mars bar or a muesli biscuit, and a drink of water. Whenever we passed a spring or stream we would have a good drink and refill our water bottles. By late morning we were ready for lunch - bread, cheese, crackers and more water, sometimes flavoured with Gatorade or Kool-aid. We would then continue to our nightstop, which we aimed to reach by mid-afternoon. The routine was then to collect water, gather firewood, unpack gear and have afternoon tea. In the warm weather we would have a good wash and often wash our socks and undies, drying them on rocks or hanging them on a length of paracord tied between two trees.

At about 5pm we would light a fire and cook our main meal of the day, which was either rice, pasta or instant potato with a sauce or can of meat/tuna. Dessert was usually dried fruit - prunes, apricots, apple, pineapple, etc. We were invariably in bed before dusk after a nightcap of hot chocolate.

As we said, life on the Trail is simple. We often wondered why we work so hard for so long to buy all the "necessities" of modern life - house with central-heating and all mod-cons, car, etc - when we feel so happy, comfortable and at peace out in the woods carrying all we need on our backs and sleeping in very basic shelters. Having said that - it is nice to know that all the creature comforts are there to go back to at the end of the adventure!

Not all days were idyllic though. Some days, when we were wet and cold and tired, we would wonder why we were doing this; but once we were snug and warm in our sleeping-bags with a comforting mug of tea or hot chocolate, life looked rosy again! Some days were made miserable by mosquitoes and blackflies, and occasionally it was so hot and humid that we felt really drained of energy and it was difficult to drag ourselves up another mountain. At times we found it rather depressing to be walking in the woods all the time - trees, trees, trees. It seemed such a waste of energy to climb to the top of a mountain and to see no view, just more trees! But, as summer approached we were glad of the shade in the forest and soon came to appreciate the occasional view as a rare gem.

But, more than compensating for the bad times, were the warm, sunny days with wild flowers blooming all around, the fresh green leaves on the trees, the cold, clear water in the streams. And all the birds and animals we saw and heard.

And maybe the greatest pleasure was meeting so many wonderful people, both on and off the Trail. Fellow hikers were great company in the shelters and hostels; and people living near the Trail were always so friendly and generous.

We met hikers of all ages on the AT, but the two main age groups seemed to be the young people who had just finished college and were taking time out before starting a career, and older people who had recently retired. Obviously to complete the entire Trail in one hike takes 5 or 6 months so is not possible for someone in a regular job, but we came across several hikers who just felt in need of a break from the "rat race" of modern life and had given up their jobs in the hope that they would find employment on their return. There were several people who had recently been made redundant and also many, like us, who had taken the opportunity of early retirement. Others, who are not in a position to risk losing secure jobs, hike the Trail a section at a time over several years. So anyone can do it if they are fit and healthy and determined. In 1990 Bill Irwin hiked the entire AT with his guide dog - Bill is blind.

We always hike as a pair and this is how we tackled the AT, but many prospective hikers have asked our opinion of solo hiking on the Trail. All we can do is reiterate the advice of the ATC who say that hiking with at least one partner reduces the risk of harassment and makes it easier to obtain help should an injury occur. Having repeated ATC's advice we must add that this applies anywhere in the world, and you are no more at risk on the AT than on any other Trail. There have been incidents, even murders, on the AT but we never felt threatened. Our personal view is that you are safer on the Trail than in most cities or on the road, so if you are comfortable hiking alone then do so; but if approached by a doubtful character pretend that you are one of a group following close behind. If you still feel unhappy, tag along with another hiker. We met many hikers travelling alone, either from preference or because they could not find a partner able to spend 6 months on the Trail. We found that as the miles were covered pairs and groups split up, and solo hikers joined with others. Even if you hike alone you will invariably meet up with others along the Trail and at shelters, especially if you set out from Springer Mountain in April.

There is an excellent "jungle telegraph" system on the Appalachian Trail based on the registers provided at shelters and other strategic points along the route. Hikers are requested to sign in at these registers, so if an emergency occurs requiring them to be contacted they can be traced very rapidly. We saw this happen on two occasions when a sudden death had occurred in a hiker's family and each time they were traced and notified in time to get home for the funeral. This is the serious side of registers, but they also provide very interesting reading in the evenings as most entries contain hikers' thoughts as they progress, hints for following hikers on places to stay (and not to stay!), good places to eat, etc as well as messages to friends who have dropped behind, poems, drawings, in fact anything that comes into the hiker's mind at the time.

Another AT tradition which you will see in the registers is that of Trail names. Obviously there are many people with similar names on the Trail at any one time, and it is difficult to recall a person after only a brief acquaintance, but an original Trail name makes them easier to remember. We were known as "The Olde Yorkies", referring to the fact that we were from "old" York (as opposed to New York). Many Trail names include a reference to the hiker's home, e.g. Indiana Dan, African Annie, Boston Bones; others to physical characteristics - Bigfoot, Daddy Long Legs, Greybeard. The scope is endless! Many hikers we met are only known to us by their Trail names.

Chapter 6

OUR PROGRESS ALONG THE TRAIL : 1990

Maryland and Pennsylvania : 28 March - 19 April.

On 28th March, a beautiful sunny day, we hiked out of Harpers Ferry, crossed the bridge over the Potomac River into Maryland and were on our way on the Appalachian Trail. Forty miles of the Trail are in Maryland, mostly following the crest of South Mountain, a long ridge running north - south. But the first 2.5 miles were very easy going along the towpath of the disused Chesapeake & Ohio Canal, after which we crossed the railroad and began our first climb to the top of Weverton Cliff. The trail was very well-graded with 14 switchbacks, and at the top we stopped for a break and enjoyed the lovely view back over the Potomac River. We stopped and chatted with two day-hikers at the road crossing in Gathland State Park, and it was strange to realise that it was only two days since we had flown in to America. We ate our lunch and treated ourselves to cans of Coke from the vending machine outside the Ranger's office. These machines were to become one of the welcome sights of the Trail, the ice-cold cans of Coke gave a real boost to hot, tired hikers! The bright red boxes were to be found outside most stores, garages, motels, etc and were always available, even when the rest of the establishment was closed. So we ensured that we always had a few quarters (25c coins) in our pockets to use, both in these machines and in payphones.

Our first night was spent at Crampton Gap shelter and, as we were early in the hiking season, we were on our own. We collected wood and lit a fire (our first ever campfire), collected water from the nearby spring, laid out our mats and sleeping-bags, and cooked our first camp meal. We were pleased to be on our own as we were such novices, but we would have liked company later when it was dark and we were aware of all the strange noises in the woods! We were in bed by 7pm, but as our body clocks were still on UK time it felt like midnight.

Before getting to sleep we heard strange rustling noises which seemed to come from inside the shelter, and we soon discovered that most of the shelters have resident families of mice. At first this was rather disconcerting, especially when they ran across our sleeping-bags during the night, or plucked at our hair (to use for nest material). We soon got used to them though, and took care to hang up our food-bag to protect it from them.

We slept well and awoke at 6am. It took us 2 hours to have breakfast, pack our gear and get back on the Trail; as time went by we got our routine refined and were usually away in about 1 hour 15 mins.

We were carrying a tent, but we made use of the shelters most of the time. They are 3-sided constructions (open at the front) made of local materials - either wood or stone. Most have a rough stone fireplace outside and an outhouse (privy) nearby.

The Appalachian Trail is well waymarked with white blazes (6"x 2" painted marks on trees or rocks) for the whole 2000 plus miles and blue blazes mark side trails to shelters, springs, viewpoints, etc. We were carrying the excellent guide-books and maps published by the ATC so navigation was no problem. The pathway itself was usually well-defined and maintained. Our first surprise was to find that we were hiking through woods with only occasional views - usually where the trees had been cut down to allow power-lines to be routed over the ridge. This was a disappointment at first as we were used to the extensive views from the ridge-tops in Britain, but we soon began to appreciate the protection provided against strong winds and, later, very hot sun. Blowdowns were a problem early in the year as many trees are felled by gales and ice-storms in the winter. In many areas we were hiking before the volunteer trail-maintainers had been out to clear the obstructions so we had to clamber over or under the fallen trees, or bushwhack round them.

As the trail is routed along the top of the ridge of the Appalachian Mountains, we crossed many roads built in the gaps in the ridge. By studying our guide-books we could plan ahead for resupply points on these roads. Occasionally there would be a grocery store near the trail crossing, but we often had to go several miles down the mountain to civilization so we soon became adept at hitch-hiking down to town and back to the trail. For most of our hike we resupplied every 4 or 5 days. As well as restocking with food we would usually spend a night in a motel or hostel so that we could shower and do our laundry.

On our fourth day on the Trail we crossed from Maryland to Pennsylvania. The previous two days had been dull and misty with light rain and we had seen no other hikers. At the weekend we met a few day-hikers, but we had the shelters to ourselves at night. One night we had to rig up the flysheet of our tent inside the shelter as the roof leaked and it rained most of the night, but we discovered that the sound of rain on the roof hid the sounds of the mice so we slept well! By morning there was about a litre of water in the flysheet, but our down sleeping-bags were dry.

About 230 miles of the Trail are in Pennsylvania and, although the mountains here are of moderate height, the walking is not easy due to the very rocky nature of the land. We had read about the Pennsylvania rocks, and the reports were not exaggerated! The further north we went, the rougher it became. In places the ridge tops are slabs of rock, some angled at 45 degrees and very slippery in the wet. In other areas the trail crosses large boulder-fields, and for many miles the path consists of small, loose, sharp rocks - rather like railway ballast. All this is very tough on boots and feet. In fact, it aggravated an old problem with John's foot and he had to visit a doctor for treatment, but it recurred later.

When we hiked through pine forests the thick carpet of soft pine needles underfoot was a real luxury, but we were shocked to find large areas of devastated oak forest. We learned later that these trees have been killed by gypsy moths which were introduced into America from Europe in the nineteenth century in an experiment to try to cross breed them with silk moths. The experiment failed and in 1869 some moths escaped from a laboratory in Massachusetts and thrived. Ever since they have gradually spread south living on the native trees and destroying the forests. Spraying with insecticide has had limited success and many people now object to this on environmental grounds. We were told that once the trees in an area are dead the moths move on and the forest is now beginning to regenerate itself, but it will be a long process. In Pennsylvania we saw the chrysalises and egg clusters on the tree trunks and in the early summer we were to see the caterpillars as far south as southern Virginia

On our seventh day on the Trail we came to Pine Grove Furnace State Park where we stayed at the AYH (American Youth Hostel). This is a beautiful old house built in 1762 for the ironmaster in charge of the charcoal furnace where local ore was smelted, using wood from the forest to provide the charcoal. Although we arrived early we were made very welcome by the houseparents (wardens), Bob and Joan Beard, who showed us around the building and told us about it's history. Apparently George Washington once stayed here (it wasn't a youth hostel then!). In the Civil War escaping slaves were sheltered in the house and we were shown the secret hiding places in the basement. Many Civil War battles took place along the route followed by the Appalachian Trail and in several places we were to see the graves of soldiers buried where they fell, many of them still carefully tended.

There was a cool breeze blowing when we left Pine Grove in

the morning and when we climbed back to the ridge it was snowing, but not settling. The next day was cool, dry and sunny as we climbed up and over three rocky ridges before dropping down to cross Yellow Breeches Creek to begin the crossing of the Cumberland Valley. At that time this was the longest road walk on the Appalachian Trail, but it has since been relocated off the roads. We enjoyed the pleasant walk through flat agricultural countryside with pretty houses and farms, although we would have appreciated somewhere to buy a cool drink or ice-cream - there wasn't even a Coke machine!

Three major roads are routed through the Cumberland Valley and after crossing the Pennsylvania Turnpike on a bridge we decided to turn off the Trail at US 11 to spend the night in a motel so that we could get a shower after a long, hot day. We were pleased that we had made this decision because on the TV that evening we saw that a belt of heavy snow was forecast to cross the area in the next couple of days. So, rather than returning to the hills next day, we took the bus into Harrisburg the State Capital of Pennsylvania.

Later in the day we tried to hitch a lift to a motel, but Jon Erdossy, the owner of a local gas-station, offered to put us up at his house. We were reluctant to impose on his family, but when we discovered that the motel had closed down we accepted his generous offer, and the Erdossys have become good friends. All the way along the Trail we found that local people were really friendly and would put themselves out to help hikers.

The snow did come, with a vengeance, even at the low level where we were staying and we later heard that a hiker was rescued from the nearby hills. After spending 3 days with Jon, his wife Diane and daughter Colleen, they put us back on the Trail at Duncannon.

When we climbed back up the ridge there was still snow lying, but the sky was blue and the sun shone, a beautiful day for hiking. We reached Peters Mountain shelter in mid afternoon and Pam volunteered to go for the water. A bad decision - the spring was a long, long way down the steep rocky hillside, it took 14 minutes to climb down, 5 minutes to fill the 7 litre waterbag and 10 minutes to climb back up again! We found this sort of situation in many places from Pennsylvania to New York State, we were hiking along the top of the rocky ridge and the spring line was way below us. The problem is worse in the summer when the springs often dry up.

We awoke early to a cold, frosty morning and were away by 7.30 for a 17.3 mile hike to the next shelter. The terrain was reasonably easy with just one steep descent of 800' followed by a long climb of 1000'. The snow was still lying and we ate handfuls of it on the climb to conserve our water supply. Back on top of the ridge we were hiking through the beautiful St. Anthony's Wilderness area and found that the trail followed an old stagecoach road through the woods. Quite a contrast to the busy modern highways we had crossed down in the valley. At Rausch Gap shelter we settled in and built a fire. When we started cooking our meal we noticed several little heads peeping out of holes between the rocks - the mice reminded us of the cute little creatures in Walt Disney cartoons! We were worried that they would keep us awake during the night as they were so bold even in daylight, but they didn't disturb us at all.

Next day found us walking through woods and passing the sites of an old railroad and coal-mining villages, but there wasn't much to see even with the guide book to alert us to the historical sites. At Swatara Gap we crossed over the creek on a 100 year old iron bridge and then went under the twin concrete flyovers of Interstate 81, another startling contrast of style and scale. Back up on the ridge we had to negotiate lots of blowdowns across the trail, and we saw our first wild turkeys and a groundhog. The last half mile of the day was very rough and rocky, and we were glad to reach our night stop just before torrential rain began. We stayed at the Blue Mountain Eagle Climbing Club hostel, a big, airy wooden shed with bunks and a huge skylight. We cooked our meal by candlelight and retired early, but were woken several times during the night by the sound of heavy rain beating on the skylight.

Next day was cool and dull, but dry. The trail was very rocky underfoot, even the gentle looking woodland paths had sharp little "teeth" lurking in them. After 13 miles we arrived at Eagles Nest shelter at 3.15pm. It is a beautiful new shelter built of huge pine logs; we had seen pictures in "Trailway News" of it being airlifted in by helicopter the previous year. From the trail it is approached over a spectacular wooden bridge over a deep gully with the stream in the bottom. Someone had obviously stopped there for lunch as the fireplace was still warm, so we soon had a good fire going and had a cup of hot chocolate made before the hailstorm started. The sun came out later, but it had turned very cold and we kept our clothes on through the night.

When we awoke at 6.20am there was a covering of snow and it was bitterly cold, but we were snug and warm and had slept well. As we were preparing breakfast we were surprised when another hiker appeared. He was Ron "Steadyfoot" Magiorre who had left Springer Mountain in January. He was the first thru-hiker of 1990 and we later heard that he completed the hike at Katahdin in June. He joined us for breakfast and told us that he had arrived at the shelter at 7.30 the previous evening and found us fast asleep so, rather than disturb us, he had slept in the woods in his bivi bag. What a gentleman! He knew who we were as he had been reading our entries in the registers all the way from Harpers Ferry as he caught up with us along the trail. He went on his way as we packed our gear and by the time we left the sun was shining.

It was an easy 9 miles along the ridge before dropping down into the small town of Port Clinton, where we arrived at noon. We needed to resupply here so we checked into the hotel, which was very old but clean and cosy. The owner, Helen Carbaugh who is her in 70s, offered to take us shopping to the nearby town of Hamburg where we also used the laundromat and the bank. We spent an interesting evening in the hotel bar chatting with Helen and the "locals".

We didn't sleep very well as we were disturbed by the noise of the traffic, a noisy radiator and the ancient, saggy iron bedstead we were sleeping in. All so different to the peace, quiet and hard wooden floors we had become used to. Next morning Helen cooked us an excellent breakfast, finishing with toast and her homemade peach jam.

The temperature was below freezing when we set out, but it was bright and sunny. We met quite a few day-hikers and soon realised that it was Good Friday. We arrived at the superb viewpoint of The Pinnacle after negotiating a very rocky trail, and were surprised to find the area swarming with tourists! We quickly ate our lunch before continuing on our way, and found that the way down was the easy tourist path to the car park. There are no shelters in this area, but we had read about a barn which is available for thru'-hikers to sleep in. After hiking 15.7 miles we arrived at the barn, which was pretty tatty but we didn't feel like going a further 10 miles to a shelter so we stayed there. Pam went into the gloomy place first and leapt back with a yell when she saw a leg hanging from the ceiling. When John investigated he found that it was an old pair of jeans with a boot attached, stuffed with rags and a note saying "This could be you, loft unsafe"! After unpacking we lit a fire outside and aired our boots and socks in the sunshine while we prepared our meal.

We overslept next day and didn't get away until 8.40am. The first 3 miles were good, easy walking but then it got very rough and we were either rock-hopping on boulders or picking our way over smaller, very hard and sharp rocks. We had only planned a short day to the next shelter, so we had a relaxing afternoon chatting with two university students who were there when we arrived. While we were preparing our dinner a day-hiker arrived and stayed for about an hour. We learnt he was Gary Kocher who had been hiking the AT in sections over several years and hoped to complete it later in the year. We later met him in Georgia as he hiked the final miles of the Trail.

It rained during the night so the rocks were wet and slippery next day as we headed for Bake Oven Knob shelter. A knife edge called "The Cliffs" was particularly tricky as it is smooth slabs inclined at an angle of about 30°, but we managed with only a few slips. When we collected water from the stream near the shelter we startled two deer which were drinking there, a reminder that even clear, cool water sources may be contaminated. Again we were joined for about an hour by some hikers just out for the day. We enjoyed their company, but had the shelter to ourselves again for the night.

After a cold start, the next day soon warmed up and we hiked in bright sunshine to Lehigh Gap. From the top of the ridge we could see the bright red of a Coke machine outside a garage, so we made good time down the rocky path to the road! The pain in John's foot had been getting worse so we planned to go into the town of Palmerton to find a doctor. We tried to get a lift from Lehigh Gap, but had no luck so we had to walk into town along the railroad as there was no footpath or verge beside the highway. After all those Pennsylvania rocks we had to walk 2 miles on railway ballast! We checked in to the only hotel in Palmerton - the Palmerton Hotel! It was pretty old and basic, and reminded us of the ones you see in old western films with a long bar where the baddies would slide the bottles of booze from one end to the other before starting to kick over the tables and smash chairs over the goodies heads! It was very quiet when we were there though!

On our way in to Palmerton we had seen a sign for a podiatrist (foot doctor), just what we needed, so next morning we went to see him. He gave John a steroid injection in his heel and a prescription for some anti-inflammatory tablets and, after a day's rest, we set off again. We had made friends with Nadine who owned the diner across the street from the Hotel and she gave us a lift back to the trail. The ridge above Palmerton looked like a moonscape as it was very rocky and had been stripped bare of trees by the pollution from the zinc smelter in town. We were pleased to hear though that work was to begin to restore the soil and vegetation.

We soon discovered that we had left our guide-book in Nadine's car, but there was nothing we could do about it so we just followed the white blazes. In the heat of the day we began to realise how much we missed the shade of the trees.

After two more days along the rocky ridge we arrived on Mount Minsi and began the long descent to Delaware Water Gap. The Delaware River forms the boundary between Pennsylvania and New Jersey, and the Appalachian Trail crosses the state line at Delaware Water Gap. The river has cut a spectacular gorge through the ridge and the AT zigzags down with superb views of the rock strata on the far side.

At Delaware Water Gap we had completed 270 miles, through two states in three weeks. It was now time to travel to Georgia and start the Trail from the beginning - Springer Mountain.

Georgia : 26 April - 2 May.

We spent a week travelling south, sampling the American public transport services - Greyhound buses and Amtrak trains - and visiting some of the friends we had made so far on our hike.

We took the overnight train from Washington to Gainesville, Georgia where we had arranged to be met at the station by Ben LaChance. He drove us to the small town of Dahlonega where we checked in to a hotel for a day and night's rest. Next morning he picked us up and drove us on rough forest roads to a point 0.9 miles north of the summit of Springer Mountain, the nearest road access to the southern terminus of the Appalachian Trail. We walked the short distance south to the summit, where we signed the register and took photographs before starting our hike north from Springer Mountain at 8.30am on 26th April.

Spring had arrived in Georgia and when we reached Hawk Mountain shelter at noon the temperature was 80°F. We had planned an easy schedule as the mountains were higher and the terrain more rugged than we were used to, but our three week "warm-up" hike had toned our bodies and we made good time. We decided to stay at the shelter as planned and met several other "thru'-hikers" who were starting their hike, but they all continued for a few more miles. So we were once again on our own. There was a notice pinned up in the shelter warning that there was a mother bear with two cubs in the area, so we hung our food bag on paracord between two trees. It is a tricky operation as bears can climb trees so the bag has to be some 12' above the ground; but the procedure was soon to become routine. We had a disturbed night, with all sorts of strange noises but we saw no bears.

We were away early next morning wearing shorts and T-shirts on a hot, sunny day. It was lovely walking through the Chattahoochee National Forest with all the new buds bursting and lots of wild flowers - violets, miniature iris and trillium. We met and passed several of the hikers we had seen the previous day as they got going later than us. We were to meet up with them many times as the days and weeks passed and the sense of kinship and camaraderie was great. We really enjoyed the social-life in the shelters and on the Trail as we had had no company at all through Maryland and Pennsylvania.

The weather was hot and humid and we stopped at streams whenever the opportunity arose to soak our feet and to refill our water bottles. We used a pump filter to purify all our drinking water as we didn't want to jeopardize our hike by contracting giardia or any other water-borne nasty. Many hikers were using iodine to treat their water, but we did not think this was wise for a long hike (up to 6 months). Some drank straight from the streams and springs (and some caught giardia).

The next day we had to detour off the Trail to the small village of Suches, as we had to pick up a package at the post office there (one of the books we had left in Nadine's car in Pennsylvania). We thumbed a lift from the first vehicle we saw, an ancient jeep, and later almost regretted it as the driver and his friend were merrily drinking cans of beer as we meandered down the mountain road! However, they dropped us safely at the door of the post office and we collected our mail. After buying drinks (non-alcoholic!) and bananas at the village store we headed back up the ridge. This time we were given a lift by a gentleman in a very smart van and we were soon back on the trail. We found a pleasant spot by a stream to set up our tent that night; it had been a good day - 15.4 miles in hot, sunny weather.

April 28th is John's birthday and we awoke at 5am to the sound of rain on the tent, so we zipped up the door and stayed in bed for another hour. We eventually set off at 8.40 in all our wet weather gear and soon joined Abe and Janet "The Austin Armadillos" from Texas, whom we had met the previous day. We hiked together in the rain to the summit of Blood Mountain which is supposed to have one of the finest views in Georgia, but all we saw was cloud. We arrived at the Walasi-Yi Center in Neel's Gap where there is a hiker hostel and store, so we all decided to stay the night. Shortly after we arrived there was a violent thunderstorm with enormous hailstones. Other hikers straggled in looking wet and bedraggled, but after a hot shower and a good meal we all celebrated John's 54th birthday and also our completion of 300 trail miles and one month on the AT.

After a hearty breakfast at the hostel we set off on another hot day, but it was really pleasant hiking in the woods where everything was green and fresh after the rain. We stopped for a rest at Low Gap shelter at 3pm and were feeling good so decided to continue to the next shelter. It was easy going at first, but then the trail became very rocky and we had to take care as we clambered over several rock slides on the steep mountain side. We were very tired by the time we arrived at Blue Mountain shelter, having hiked 18 miles in 11 hours. Kevin, another of the hikers we had met previously, was already at the shelter and had gathered a bag full of edible wild plants which he gave us to supplement our dehydrated packet meal. The mixture of fresh leaves (violet, mint, etc) was delicious and made us realise how much we missed fresh vegetables.

Next day, after hiking 13 hot miles we arrived at Addis Gap shelter, situated in a beautiful valley one third of a mile off the trail. There was a cool stream flowing past the shelter so we washed our socks and had a refreshing bathe before cooking our meal. We were again joined by Kevin and Jeff, who had been with us at Neel's Gap, and we spent a pleasant evening chatting.

One piece of advice we had noted was that in the southern mountains thunderstorms frequently develop by mid-afternoon. So we planned to set out early and arrive at shelters by 3pm if possible. This ploy worked really well; we had often just got ourselves settled in when a storm broke but we were dry and comfortable with our afternoon cup of tea. Other hikers would arrive later looking very wet and miserable. Another advantage of this regime was that we were usually the first to arrive at a shelter and if it rained we could see where the roof leaked before choosing the spot for our bed! We were still able to average 15 miles a day and would feel more rested and refreshed than if we had continued until 5 or 6pm.

This strategy was proved correct the next day. We hiked 10 miles to Plumorchard Gap shelter and arrived there with Jeff just after

3pm. It had been hot and humid all day and we had just returned from collecting our water when we heard the wind come roaring up the valley behind the shelter. In no time the storm broke with torrential rain, thunder and lightening. Fortunately all our gear was under cover and we remained dry, but the suddenness of the storm would have given little opportunity to seek shelter if we had been out on the trail.

We were in bed by 8pm, but were awoken later by a growl nearby. Our first thought was "bears", but then a dog appeared in front of the shelter! It was Godiva, a chocolate labrador, and her owner Terry, a lawyer from Washington. We had met them earlier, but they had been delayed when they were caught in the storm and had then had to hike in the dark to reach the shelter for the night.

Despite the previous evening's disturbance, we were up at 6am and on the trail by 7.30. It was cooler and fresher after the storm and we enjoyed walking through the woods, where the first azaleas were in bloom and we saw lady's slipper orchids flowering beside the trail.

Tennessee and North Carolina : 2 May - 1 June.

At Bly Gap we crossed into North Carolina and the Nantahala National Forest, an area of high mountains with 5,000' peaks and 4,000' gaps. This was Indian country until the Cherokees were driven out in 1838, but many of the picturesque local names date from that era. We stopped for lunch at Muskrat Creek shelter and then continued to Standing Indian shelter where we arrived at 3.15pm after hiking 12.3 miles. There was a lovely stream flowing by so we had a good bathe, and had a fire going before Jeff arrived. The storm came later than usual that afternoon. We had eaten our meal and just finished the washing-up when the thunder started. Terry and Godiva arrived just before the storm really broke; but Abe and Janet came in, drenched, at 6.30. So we re-arranged our sleeping-bags to make room for everybody. Godiva started barking during the night, and Abe thought he could smell skunk, so Terry brought the dog inside the shelter to avoid a confrontation. It was a snug fit in the shelter that night!

Next morning was cool and overcast and we made good time on a well-graded trail. We had hiked 12 miles by the time we stopped for lunch at noon, then came the climb to the summit of Albert Mountain (5250'). This was most enjoyable with a scramble over rocks for the final quarter mile. At the start of the rocky area we came across a garter snake lying across the trail. It would not move away despite banging our stick on the rocks and rustling the leaves near it, so we had to flick it into the undergrowth with a stick. It scurried away then! Despite being hazy the view from the fire tower on top of the mountain was very spectacular.

Although we were now at heights above 5000' we were still hiking through the forest with beautiful flowering shrubs - rhododendron, magnolia, viburnum, dogwood, etc. - even on the top of Albert Mountain. We were also seeing deer and hearing woodpeckers, grouse and other birds which we could not recognise. We saw bear droppings on the trail, but no bears, and saw many non-poisonous garter and black rat snakes. Although there are timber rattlesnakes in the area, we saw none.

We were spending the night with Abe, Janet and Jeff at Big Spring shelter, just below the summit of Albert Mountain, when we were awakened shortly after midnight by torrential rain, thunder and lightening. This frightening storm continued until 4.30am, with hail thrown in for good measure. At times it was almost like daylight as we were in the cloud and the continuous lightening illuminated the whole area. Needless to say, we didn't get much sleep that night but we did keep dry and warm.

Despite our lack of sleep we were all up at 6.30am. It was still raining, but Abe went out and unhooked all the food bags from the trees so we could have breakfast. By the time we were packed and ready to go it had stopped raining and we all set off together. We had a brisk 6-mile hike to Wallace Gap where we planned to walk down the road to Rainbow Springs Campground. Just as we reached the road the truck from the campground arrived to put some hikers back on the trail, so we got a lift which saved us a mile on the tarmac. The five of us rented a cabin for the night and spent a restful day doing our laundry and buying fresh supplies at the camp store. Terry and Godiva arrived later and stayed in the bunkhouse.

Next morning Abe cooked spicy Texas omelettes and bacon for us all for breakfast. A real feast! Then we got a lift back to the trail and were hiking by 9 o'clock. It was a mild day with a cool wind, ideal hiking weather and we made good time, arriving at the first shelter by noon. So after eating our lunch we decided to continue to the next shelter, making a total of 19.3 miles for the day, including a beautiful hike over Wayah Bald (5,336') with superb views from the observation tower on the summit. We arrived at Cold Spring shelter at 5.20pm to find it already full with the hikers who had left Rainbow Springs the previous day.

We were feeling quite tired by then so we continued a short distance past the shelter and put up our tent. Abe and Janet arrived later and put up their tent beside ours, but Jeff managed to squeeze into the shelter with the others. The wind was very chilling and the cloud came down, so we cooked our dinner and closed ourselves in the tent for the evening. We soon became aware of a strange thumping sound, but thought it was probably the U.S. Army on exercise in the area as we had seen military vehicles at a road crossing earlier in the day. We learned later that it was the drumming sound made by the ruffed grouse in their courtship display!

It was cold and very windy during the night, and we awoke to find the tent stiff with frost. But once on the trail the weather soon warmed up with a clear blue sky and we had to stop and change into our shorts. There were lovely views when we came out of the trees on top of Wesser Bald (4,627') and then a wonderful panoramic view from a rocky outcrop called Jump Up. Next came the long, steep descent of nearly 3,000' in 4 miles to the Nantahala River at Wesser, where the Nantahala Outdoor Center has a motel and hostel. We booked a room for two nights in the motel and enjoyed the facilities of this canoeing and white water rafting centre, especially the excellent restaurants! Jeff, Terry, Abe and Janet also stayed there, so we had a very sociable weekend with our friends.

We were running short of cash at this stage, so one of the girls in the motel office offered to drive us to Bryson City to visit a bank and also resupply at the supermarket. On our return we went to the cafeteria for lunch and were approached by a couple at the next table who had heard us talking. They had recognised our English accents and assumed we must be "The Olde Yorkies" - they had been behind us all the way from Springer and had been reading our entries in the registers so they felt they already knew us. They joined us at our table and we learned that they were Linda and Jim who had set off from Springer Mountain (independently) two days after us. When Jim signed the register at the start of the AT he noticed Linda's name there and thought "I used to date a Linda White at school". Later that day they met at Hawk Mountain shelter and he discovered that it was the same person he had dated and had not seen or heard of for 24 years! That is what we call "Trail Magic" - something completely unexpected that adds a touch of magic to the Appalachian Trail experience.

Next morning we were waiting outside the cafeteria with most of the other hikers when the doors opened at 7am. After breakfast we all set off in ones and twos, and "leap-frogged" one another most of the day. We stopped at Sassafras Gap shelter for lunch and were joined by Linda, Jim and Jeff. After filling our water bottles at a spring we climbed to the top of Cheoah Bald (5,062') where we admired our first view of the Great Smoky Mountains. Along this section we met up with a group of U.S. Army rangers on exercise. We later spent several nights with them through the Smokies and found them to be great company, especially as they shared their MREs ("meals ready to eat") with us! It was also very encouraging to find that we were doing the same daily mileage as they were, although they were carrying 70-100lbs and we only had 40lbs each.

The trail in this area was very rugged with many ups and downs and was quite tiring in the heat, but we hiked 13 miles before putting up our tent at the foot of the long descent into Stecoah Gap. We were soon joined by Jeff, Linda and Jim who all put up their tents nearby as we all felt too tired to tackle the climb up out of the Gap. We slept well despite being disturbed occasionally by traffic passing on the road.

We awoke to light rain, which got heavier as the day progressed. It was a tiring day, with two steep climbs and lots of ups and downs. When we arrived at Cable Gap shelter for our lunch break, we found it full of the Army lads, but they made room for us and even lent us two folding stools to sit on! We rested there for 40 minutes and then continued along the trail which was by now very wet and slippery, especially on the narrow path which zigzagged down the mountainside to the road at Fontana.

We must have looked really wet and bedraggled as we walked the 2 miles along the road to the motel at Peppertree Village, it was hardly surprising that nobody stopped to give us a lift. At the motel we were handed the key to Room 104, which turned out to be the Appalachian Suite! This was most luxurious, with a pale blue carpet - not really appropriate for two dripping hikers in muddy boots, but when we had showered and put on clean clothes we really appreciated our comfortable surroundings.

Later we met Terry in reception and he told us that he was sharing a cabin with Abe and Janet. So we all met later for a meal after doing our usual chores at the laundromat and grocery store. We also discovered the ice cream parlour which served wonderful milk shakes and ice cream sundaes, so that was a good place to pass the time while the laundry did its thing next door!

We had bought enough food for the 8 day hike through the Smokies, so next morning our heavy packs were bulging when we set off. The sun was shining and it was pleasantly warm as we crossed the Fontana Dam, 480' above the Little Tennessee River. This huge dam was built by the Tennessee Valley Authority during World War II to provide hydro-electric power. It holds back the 29 mile Fontana Lake and provides a dramatic entrance to the Great Smoky Mountains National Park. The Appalachian Trail meanders for 70 miles through the Park over spectacular mountains at heights between 4,000' and 6,600', and for nearly 200 miles the Trail straddles the North Carolina/Tennessee state line along the crest of the ridge.

Black bears are prevalent in the Smokies and have become a nuisance as they have learned that hikers gather at shelters and carry food with them. So the shelters in the Park are rather different to those in other areas. They are larger than we had met so far, built of stone with wooden sleeping platforms on 2 levels to accommodate 12 hikers, with a stone fireplace inside and heavy steel mesh fences across the front to keep the bears out. You are advised to use the shelters and not camp out in tents - although some hikers, including some of the soldiers, did camp out if the shelters were crowded. We saw plenty of bear dung on the trail and around the shelters, but we were disappointed to see no bears.

The 2,000' climb up from the valley was achieved without much difficulty, but it was very windy near the top of the ridge so we had to stop and put on our windproof jackets before continuing the final mile to Birch Spring shelter.

While John was pumping water near the shelter he met a National Park ranger who was the official hog catcher. Apparently wild boar were introduced many years ago for hunting, but the population of their descendants in the Park has increased so much that a programme of culling had been introduced. We saw no hogs during our hike, but we saw signs of their presence where they had been rooting in the soft soil beside the trail.

There were lots of hikers in the Park though, most were just out for a few days or a week. This put a lot of pressure on the shelter accommodation. There were 13 of us in the shelter that first night, which was OK; but one of our companions snored very loudly so we didn't sleep very well.

We were very lucky to have warm, sunny weather for our hike through the Smoky Mountains. The scenery was beautiful, but the trail was much more eroded than we had seen before. On our second day in the Park we arrived at Spence Field shelter before noon and stopped there for lunch. It is in a beautiful position just off the trail, and the serviceberry trees were in full bloom all around. While we were having lunch we watched a red squirrel searching for crumbs around the shelter, and an inquisitive deer came right up to us to investigate. The animals are obviously used to humans around here and are very tame.

John's foot had been painful during the morning hike so we decided to spend the night at this beautiful shelter. We sunbathed on the grass in the afternoon and other hikers arrived. Some just stopped for a break and then continued, but several decided to stay, so we soon had a full shelter again. Some of the soldiers were with us and we spent a sociable evening around a big campfire.

There was some rain during the night and it was quite windy

next morning, but good weather for hiking. We were amazed at all the trees in blossom at this high level, it was often like walking through a beautiful orchard with views of mountains all around us. We were going up and down mountains all day - Thunderhead (5,527'), Cold Spring Knob (5,240') and Silers Bald (5,607'). We were the first to arrive at Double Spring Gap shelter, but were soon joined by several of our companions of the previous night.

Next morning was foggy as we hiked towards Clingmans Dome, at 6,643' it is the highest point on the Appalachian Trail, and we were in the cloud so missed the views. We were aware, though, of vast areas of dead trees looking very eerie in the mist. We learned later that they had been killed by the effects of acid rain, something we had never seen at first hand before. It was most depressing to see that, even in this remote spot, man's pollution is destroying the environment.

We continued to Newfound Gap, the only road crossing in the Smokies, and found several military vehicles in the parking area. They were there to collect our Army friends who were to leave the Trail at this point. As they packed their equipment into the trucks they gave us all the remaining food supplies, so our rucksacks were again bulging! After eating our lunch and saying our goodbyes, we continued on our way, stopping to take a nostalgic photograph at the AT sign which had first made us aware of the existence of the Appalachian Trail.

The fog had cleared and the sun was shining, so we had a pleasant 3 mile hike to the next shelter at Icewater Spring. There were four people already installed at the shelter, and hikers continued to arrive throughout the afternoon. By the time we had lit a fire and cooked our meal there were 18 of us at the shelter built for 12. We managed to fit in all the sleeping-bags - it was going to be very cosy!

It was a nice, mild evening so we sat outside chatting with some of the other hikers, including Ann Cuddy and daughter who were spending a week in the Smokies. They live near the AT in Connecticut and they invited us to visit them when we reach that area. When we were all in bed three more people arrived so there were finally 21 of us in a shelter built for 12. There were also reported to be two resident skunks at this shelter, but we didn't see them - maybe it was too crowded for them that night!

Next morning we were away before 7am as we were attempting to hike 20 miles, missing out a shelter, and hopefully get ahead of the crowd. We hiked in perfect weather through beautiful scenery including a spectacular rock ledge walk round Charlie's Bunion, followed by the sharp crest of The Sawteeth. We stopped for lunch at Tri-Corner Knob shelter and then continued as planned to spend the night at Cosby Knob shelter. We were the first to arrive there so we collected water from the spring and had refreshing body washes which revitalised us after our long hike. Only two others arrived, so we had managed to get ahead of the crowd. In the register there were reports of frequent sightings of bear at this shelter, so we closed ourselves in the cage with our camera at the ready, but none came. The only wildlife we saw were mice!

We were now reaching the northern end of the Great Smoky Mountains National Park. It was a long, gradual descent of 3,000' in about 8 miles to Davenport Gap shelter and then a lovely walk beside a pretty, tumbling cascade, before emerging from the woods to cross the Pigeon River on a big concrete bridge. We began to appreciate how much shade is provided by the trees along the trail as it was uncomfortably hot out in the open on the concrete roadway. We then had a long, hot climb of 3,000' up Snowbird Mountain before descending again to arrive at Groundhog Creek shelter at 4.30pm. During the night a mouse gnawed a hole in our food bag, but only nibbled at the remains of a packet of nuts so no great harm was done. This was the only occasion that an animal managed to get at our provisions during the entire hike.

We were away by 7.20am and had a long climb up through the woods, with masses of colourful flowers, fresh green leaves on the trees and birds singing. Then we came to Max Patch, a beautiful grassy bald with views all around, before starting down again through woods with lovely streams tumbling down beside the trail. Although the Smokies were beautiful and we had had dry, sunny weather we had found the area too busy and we were glad to have left the National Park and returned to the quieter backwoods.

We stopped at Roaring Fork shelter for lunch, but it was so beautiful we decided to stay there for the night. It was a brand new shelter (in fact it hadn't been officially "opened") in a lovely situation in a wooded valley. Brass plaques on the wall stated that the shelter had been built by the Carolina Mountain Club, but donated by the Mountain Marching Mamas. Intriguing! While we were eating our lunch two of the "Mamas" arrived to inspect the new shelter and we learned that they were a group of ladies who enjoyed hiking in the area and had decided that a new shelter was required, so they set about raising the money to buy the materials. Another example of the generosity of local people along the Appalachian Trail.

We slept well, but were surprised to hear mice scampering around during the night - they had already taken up residence in the new shelter! It was raining when we awoke and by the time we were ready to leave it was thundering and lightening as well so we sat around until 8.30am when the storm seemed to be moving away. We set off in the rain with three other hikers who had spent the night with us. By mid morning the rain had stopped and the sun came out so we were again hiking in shorts and T-shirts.

We stopped for lunch before descending the ridge to the small town of Hot Springs in North Carolina where we had arranged to take a few days off and meet up with our friends, Joan and Fred. They live in South Carolina, but we met them in Scotland when we were hiking the West Highland Way. Unfortunately, John's foot had been giving trouble again so we had to spend one day travelling 40 miles to Asheville Hospital, where he was given a steroid injection in his heel. We then spent a pleasant couple of days resting and sightseeing with our friends before setting off on the AT again. We didn't have to go far to get back to the Trail - it goes straight down the main street, with the white blazes carefully painted on lamp posts and electricity poles!

For the next five days we continued to follow the North Carolina/Tennessee state-line along the top of the ridge, with steep ups and downs over mountains. The weather was mixed, but wet days were followed by hot, sunny ones so we were able to dry out. The trail was often wet and this brought out lots of little bright orange salamanders. We also saw several snakes and a box turtle.

There were spectacular views into the gorge before the steep descent to the Nolichucky River. The bridge across the river was closed for reconstruction work, so the AT had been detoured 4 miles towards the town of Erwin, Tennessee. After walking along the busy highway we decided to continue into town where we arrived at 11.00am and checked in to a friendly family run hotel. We did our usual chores of laundry and resupply before spending the afternoon resting in our room.

Next morning we took a taxi back to the Trail and called in at a rafting camp on the river to buy fuel for our stove. There we met Tim, a hiker we had first met on Springer Mountain but hadn't seen since Wesser, so we set off up the trail with him and he hiked with us for most of the next 3 weeks.

After climbing up Unaka Mountain we descended to Low Gap where we came across a group of horse riders dressed in "cowboy" gear. As we started the climb up out of the gap it was obvious that the horses had ridden down the AT as the steep climb was very slippery, muddy and smelly. We were very tired when we arrived at Cherry Gap shelter after hiking 15 miles. We were soon joined by Terry and his dog Godiva, and later three hikers out on a four day camping trip arrived and put up their tent near the shelter. When we were preparing and eating our meal the campers joined us and brought with them a bottle of bourbon which was handed round. As we were getting ready for bed another hiker arrived and we all finally retired by 8.30pm. It had been a warm, sunny morning, but it became overcast in the afternoon and started to rain just as we went to bed. Shortly afterwards there was a great commotion when the three campers rushed into the shelter as their tent was leaking badly. So we all moved up to make room and nine of us (plus a dog) fitted into the 6 person shelter.

It rained all night but had stopped by the time we got up at 6am. It was another tough day with the climb of 2200' up Roan Mountain in the afternoon. The trail was still wet after the overnight rain and we had to be careful not to tread on all the little salamanders underfoot. We arrived at Roan High Knob shelter just before 4pm. At 6,285' this is the highest shelter on the AT and is, in fact, an enclosed 2 storey cabin which was originally built to accommodate the local forest ranger. We got a good fire going with a supply of wood which had been left on the porch, and were later joined by three other hikers. Terry and Godiva arrived much later as Terry had pulled a muscle and had been very slow up the mountain.

We awoke to low cloud, which continued all morning as we hiked over three balds which, we are told, have spectacular views. It was also very windy and rain started mid morning, so it was pretty miserable hiking weather. The sun eventually came out about 2pm, but the trail was very slippery and we had to watch where we put our feet. John managed to walk into a large tree which had blown down across the path at head height. It knocked him on his back with his arm trapped under his rucksack, but no damage was done apart from a headache.

When we reached a road crossing we decided to go to the

nearby town and we spent the night at the Roan Mountain Motel. We were given the room where Elvis had once stayed (complete with "Elvis" bedspreads and what was probably the original '60s wallpaper!), wonderful food though and we were made very welcome by the owner "Jersey John".

After an excellent breakfast we were given a lift back to the Trail by Jersey John. It was raining again as we set off hiking up the road and we managed to miss the AT sign directing us into the woods, so we wasted about 30 minutes before we found the right path. There had been a land dispute going on in this area between the ATC and some local landowners so hikers had been warned not to camp in the area and not to hike through alone. We had heard that a shelter had been burned down and fish-hooks had been strung across the trail at eye level, but we had no trouble, and we are not aware of any hikers having been harassed.

It was easy terrain with rolling hills and even fields of cattle - it reminded us of England - but the trail was very wet and slippery. We sat down for lunch with Tim on wet leaves under wet rhododendron bushes and then continued in the mist and rain. Pam was leading, but when we came to a tricky stream crossing Tim took the lead and promptly lost his footing on a slippery boulder and fell in the water. Fortunately no damage was done and we continued on our way, arriving at Moreland Gap shelter at 4.30pm. Three hikers had been there all day as their tent had leaked the previous night and they were trying to get dried out.

We quickly changed into dry clothes and made cups of tea as we soon got chilled when we stopped walking. When we had eaten we set out our beds and found that the rain was dripping through the roof, so we covered our sleeping-bags with our emergency blanket. The rain stopped in the evening though and the next day was dry and bright.

The sun was shining as we followed the trail down the steep, rocky side of Laurel Fork Gorge to Laurel Falls, which were magnificent after all the rain. Although only 40' high these falls are in a spectacular setting with the walls of the gorge rising 1200' on either side. We had read that the rough path at the foot of the cliffs beside the creek could be impassable after rain, but the water was just lapping the rocks so we carefully picked our way through and then climbed back up to the rim of the gorge where we sat and ate our lunch.

We were planning to stay at a hostel near Hampton, Tennessee but when we arrived there we found that it was undergoing renovation work, so we took a taxi to the next town of Elizabethton and checked in at the new Comfort Inn. This was very smart, but we were made really welcome by the manager who even did our laundry for us while we went out for a meal.

The next day was again mild and bright, and the sun came out mid morning as we hiked high above Watauga Lake - the scenery reminded us of the Lake District. We hiked 20 miles that day and when we arrived at Double Springs shelter we found not only Tim there, but also Jeff whom we hadn't seen since Hot Springs. So we spent a very pleasant evening comparing notes on our respective experiences along the trail.

The next day we hiked 18 miles and made very good time on easy terrain through woods with azaleas and mountain laurel in full bloom. We disturbed several ruffed grouse which exploded from the undergrowth at our feet, flapping noisily to distract us from their young. We also saw two wild turkeys, before crossing the stateline into Virginia and then descending to the town of Damascus.

Virginia and West Virginia : 1 June - 10 July.

One quarter of the Appalachian Trail (approx. 540 miles) is in the state of Virginia, passing through Jefferson National Forest and George Washington National Forest before reaching the Shenandoah National Park.

On 1st June we arrived in the small town of Damascus, where the AT goes along the main street and the residents make hikers very welcome. We had arranged for some replacement equipment and the Virginia guide-book and maps to be sent to us at the post office; so we were surprised (and shocked) to find that no mail had arrived for us. Fortunately we had planned to spend a night in town, so we found a room at a private house (there is a hostel but no hotels in Damascus). After settling in and bathing we went to explore town and managed to get our hair cut - very civilized. Next morning we went to the laundromat and then to the post office where we found that our parcel had arrived. What a relief!

We met several other hikers who were taking a few days off in Damascus, most of them were staying at The Place, a hostel owned by the Methodist Church. Terry was there, but he was suffering from a badly swollen foot and after visiting a doctor he came off the Trail and returned home. We heard later that he had to have surgery to cure the foot problem.

We decided to spend a second night in town as John's foot was needing a rest. Next morning there was a torrential thunderstorm just as we were ready to leave so we sat around in the diner with Tim and Jeff until the weather cleared. So after a late start we only hiked 9.5 miles on a very wet trail to the Saunders shelter, set in a beautiful pine-grove.

It again started raining just as we were ready to set out the next morning so we waited awhile to see how the weather would develop. By

8am it was clearing so we were on our way and we had a pleasant 17 mile hike in fine weather. We paralleled Laurel Creek for quite a while, walking along an old railroad bed and crossing the creek on a long disused wooden railway bridge. As we climbed away from the creek we came out above treeline and had good views from Buzzard Rock and White Top Mountain, then we dropped down to a road crossing at Elk Garden - a beautiful grassy area with masses of wild flowers in bloom. Finally we climbed up to Deep Gap shelter in a lovely wooded glade where a pretty doe was feeding when we arrived.

It was cold and damp next morning as we awoke to fog, so we didn't hang around - we were on the trail before 7am. We walked through a herd of wild ponies on the slopes of Mount Rogers, they gave us quite a start as they appeared out of the mist! The fog soon burnt off and by 10 o'clock the sun was shining and it was a beautiful day for hiking. We stopped for a snack at Old Orchard shelter and then continued through the afternoon to Raccoon Branch shelter. This area of Virginia had been badly damaged by Hurricane Hugo the previous September, but the volunteers had done a wonderful job clearing blowdowns and rebuilding miles of trail.

There followed another beautiful day with good terrain and warm, sunny weather. We stopped at the visitor centre at the Mount Rogers Recreation Area and made good use of their Coke machine and restrooms, before continuing to Chatfield shelter where we arrived just before 5pm having hiked almost 20 miles. There was a beautiful stream flowing past the front of the shelter so we had a nice refreshing bathe before cooking our meal. There were lots of biting insects around though so we had to use our insect repellent and cover our arms and legs. Five other hikers arrived so we had a full shelter.

We didn't sleep very well as we were too hot inside our sleeping-bags, and too cold outside them! But next day we only had a short 4.6 mile walk to Atkins and on the way we stopped to pick wild strawberries growing beside the trail. As we approached Atkins we were crossing grassy pastures with lots of stiles, all awkward to negotiate with big packs, but we soon arrived at the motel where we planned to take a day off for laundry, etc. Before checking in we went to the restaurant for a huge breakfast, and later one of the motel staff gave us a lift to the grocery store and laundromat.

In the afternoon we had a good rest and caught up on some of the sleep we had missed the previous night. John then did some repairs on his rucksack as the frame was wearing through the fabric at the base of the pack, and cleaned and waxed the boots before we went out to dinner with four other hikers who had arrived at the motel.

After another huge breakfast in the restaurant our day started with a hike along the highway and under the flyover of the Interstate. We soon turned off and climbed a stile into more pasture land and soon realised that the trail bore little resemblance to the description in the guide book. We followed the blazes and eventually came to a notice explaining that the AT had been relocated and the new route had only opened 6 days ago.

It was a very hot day and we stopped whenever we saw water to refill our water bottles. There were many blowdowns in this area, most had been cleared but many were still across the trail and on several occasions we had to take off our packs in order to slide under them. We stopped for lunch at a picnic pavilion beside a road and while there a couple arrived to prepare for a barbecue that night. They invited us to stay for the party, but we declined as it was a steep climb to Knot Maul Branch shelter and we did not want to do it in the dark. We filled our 7 litre water bag as the guide book told us that there is no water supply at the shelter, and then set off on the slow, hot climb. Several of the hikers who had been at the motel with us arrived later, but some continued to camp further along the trail where there was a water supply.

We had a bad night at Knot Maul Branch shelter where we heard our first whippoorwill - it serenaded us with it's piercing song just outside the shelter for most of the night. In addition, one of our fellow hikers snored. Not a gentle, rhythmical snore; but a whole repertoire of farmyard noises! We decided to buy earplugs at the next town - they have been an essential piece of our kit ever since!

We were again away before 7am, having slept badly, and had a hard hike with lots of stiff climbs. We had an early lunch at Chestnut Knob shelter which is on a lovely bald with lots of wild flowers and a spring-fed pond where we replenished our water bottles. The weather was very hot in the afternoon and the final mountain of the day was very rocky - it reminded us of Pennsylvania. The 4.5 miles along it's ridge took us 3 hours, and half way along we heard thunder. It rumbled all around and, just as we thought it had missed us, the rain started and we had to get our waterproofs on pretty quickly. For the rest of the day we hiked in intermittent rain and dripping trees, and arrived at Jenkins shelter at 6pm after a 20 mile hike. Just after we arrived, while John was collecting water, the storm really broke with torrential rain. Tim arrived in the middle of the storm - singing "Singing in the Rain"! There were ten of us there that night, but five young lads put up their tents so it wasn't too crowded.

The rain continued through the night, but we slept well and were up at 6am. The rain had stopped by the time we set out, but the trees and undergrowth were very wet. We took the alternate "High Water Route" described in the guide book as the regular route crosses Little Wolf Creek thirteen times and can be waist deep after rain. Tim caught up with us while we were having our lunch break, he had taken his chance with the creek and had fallen in at the final crossing! Fortunately the weather was warm and sunny by then and he dried out quickly. He hiked the rest of the way with us to Helveys Mill shelter where we lit a fire and hung up the wet clothes to dry. Tim caught some crayfish in the creek while he was collecting water so he cooked them with his dinner. Later a party of ten locals arrived on an evening stroll and stopped to chat with us for about 20 minutes.

The weather was ideal for hiking the next day, warm and sunny with a nice breeze. We met a U.S. Forest Service ranger at a road crossing and stopped to chat with him for a while, before continuing to Jenny Knob shelter where we met up with Tim for lunch. In the afternoon we took a detour to a grocery store where we ate cheeseburgers, pie and ice-cream and drank milk. We stayed there for an hour before returning to the trail to climb up beside Dismal Creek to Wapiti shelter. We had bought some cookies and cans of beer at the store, so we spent a pleasant evening around the campfire with Tim and another hiker who was already at the shelter when we arrived.

Tim had bought some eggs and bacon at the store so next morning we had a cooked breakfast - a real treat, although the scrambled eggs were a bit charred! We set off later than usual and had a pleasant hike along the ridge where we took photographs from a rocky outcrop with views over the Wilburn and New River valleys. The trail then became rough and rocky which slowed us down and was very uncomfortable on the feet. We passed a side trail to the Woodshole Hostel, which is an old homestead belonging to Tillie Wood who opens her home to hikers. This had been highly recommended to us, but as we had only gone 6 miles we couldn't justify stopping, so we continued on our way to Doc's Knob shelter where we stopped for lunch.

For the next 2 miles the Trail followed an old road through rhododendron and azalea before turning right and climbing steeply up the ridge beside some powerlines to reach the crest of Pearis Mountain (3,440'). We then had easy walking along an even path and soon reached an overhanging rock ledge with a view across the valley to the point where we had taken photographs in the morning. The trail had gone round in a big horseshoe! We stopped to admire the extensive views from Angels Rest (3,550') and then began the long, steep, rough descent through rhododendrons to the town of Pearisburg where we hitched a lift in a pick-up truck to a motel.

Tim waited with us in our motel room until his brother, who lives near Pearisburg, came to collect him. As we were planning to spend two nights in town, Tim and Harry offered to collect us in the morning to take us shopping in Blacksburg. So after they left we did our laundry and visited the post office where we collected several letters and a parcel containing some replacement boots for John. We then wrote letters and postcards, packaged up the old boots and also our water pump which had been very unreliable, and returned to the post office to mail them. After an excellent meal at the Virginian Restaurant we retired to bed at 10.30pm, it had been a busy day.

Having completed our chores the previous evening we were free to enjoy a day off with Tim and Harry. They drove us 20 miles to Blacksburg where we visited Blue Ridge Outdoors store, which stocks a large selection of hiking and backpacking equipment. We bought several small items which needed replacing, and also a Katadyn water filter to replace the Filopur which had let us down. The staff were extremely helpful and even phoned round to other shops to locate items which they didn't stock. They also recommended a person who may be able to repair John's rucksack, so we visited the lady cobbler before going to a Chinese restaurant for lunch. On our return we found that she had done an excellent job of enclosing the frame in thick leather before rebuilding the base with soft leather patches. All for $10 - what value!

Next morning Harry brought Tim back to the motel and then returned us all to the Trail. It was warm and misty as we set off hiking at 7.10am, but it soon became hot and humid. From the top of the ridge there were good open areas with views into West Virginia, but it was all very hazy. We found a patch of shade under a tree for our lunch break and then continued down a very rocky trail which upset John's foot again. The guide book gave the distance from Pearisburg to Pine Swamp

Branch shelter as 18.2 miles, but 1.3 miles before the shelter we came to a relocation which added 1.5 miles to the total distance. After a long, hard day this was very tiring.

When we arrived at the shelter we found the Konnarock Crew based there while they worked on the relocation which, we learned, was to remove a steep, rocky descent. These volunteers had given up their time to work on major trail maintenance projects organised by ATC, living on the job for several days, weeks or months as their time allowed. There are similar groups in other areas along the Appalachian Trail giving many thousands of hours of volunteer labour each year. As the crew were sleeping in tents there was plenty of room for us in the shelter, which was a beautiful stone structure with an inside fireplace. Unfortunately we were too tired to really appreciate it, so we cooked a quick meal and retired to bed.

We were awoken by a thunderstorm which lasted for about an hour during the night, but got back to sleep and awoke at 6am. Shortly afterwards the work crew arrived and shared their melon with us as they cooked their breakfast. They were a very pleasant group of people and Tim decided to stay behind for a couple of hours and do some work with them as we were only planning a 12 mile day. The weather was dull, humid and damp when we set off at 7.45am and we made good time for the first 4 miles. The trail then became rocky and it started raining heavily so this slowed us down. After a long, steep descent we arrived at War Spur Branch shelter at 2.45pm, where we unpacked, washed and had a cup of tea before Tim arrived later.

As we left next morning and crossed the stream in front of the shelter John slipped off a rock and got both boots full of water. Not a good start to the day! Much of the morning was spent hiking through dense rhododendron growth over John's Creek Mountain, then descended through pasture and over stiles until we reached a road in the valley. We took a short detour along the road to a church pavilion which was mentioned in our guide book, where we had our lunch and refilled our water bottles.

The morning had been overcast and humid, but the sun was out as we set off again in the afternoon and climbed up through open pasture where we saw a big black snake. We crossed a field full of ox-eye daisies before climbing back into the woods to hike along the crest of Sinking Creek Mountain. This was very rocky with sloping slabs which was very tiring as it was hot and humid. After hiking 18.5 miles we arrived at Niday shelter at 5.45pm to find three people already here. Tim and two other hikers arrived later and, as we knew that one of them snored loudly, we decided to put up our tent away from the shelter. This was a good move as we could hear the snorer from 20 yards away when we roused during the night!

The next day it was again hot and humid. We found that the AT had recently been relocated over Brush Mountain and was very well graded with easy switchbacks, so was probably easier although a mile longer than the guide book description. John's foot was very painful on the long descent so we bathed our feet in Trout Creek while we ate our lunch and discussed whether to continue up and over the next mountain. The guide book said that the next few miles were very rocky and steep, so we decided to take the road which was marked on the map.

By now it was noon and it was very hot walking on the road, so we were glad to accept a lift in the back of a pick-up truck. This saved us 5 miles of road walking and was very refreshing. We were dropped at Catawba grocery store where we had arranged to meet Tim in the afternoon before climbing to the next shelter, so we went inside and bought food and drinks. We took these to a picnic table beside a nearby pond and discussed what we were going to do. John's foot had been getting progressively more painful, even after two steroid injections, and we reluctantly accepted the fact that we would be unable to hike the whole Appalachian Trail.

It was 17th June and we had hiked 942 miles. We were very disappointed and were not prepared to give up completely, so we decided to take a week off and hire a car to see if the rest would cure the problem. After two nights in a motel we felt we had to get out in the woods again, so we drove to a U.S. Forest Service campsite and put up our tent!

By the end of the week we knew that we would not be able to finish the Trail, but we decided to attempt to complete 1000 miles. So we headed north to Shenandoah National Park where we knew that the terrain was gentle and the trail well-graded with shelters every 10 miles or so. In fact it is often called the "Racetrack" as many thru'-hikers do 25 mile days through Shenandoah, but it is a shame to rush as the scenery and views are so beautiful.

We continued on the Trail from Rockfish Gap on 26th June, planning to hike about 10 miles a day from shelter to shelter. After eight days rest the climb up out of the gap was hard work, our legs felt like lead going up and like jelly going down! But we arrived at Calf Mountain shelter at 11.40am without mishap on a clear, sunny day and then spent a restful afternoon.

Bears are a problem in Shenandoah, as in the Smokies, but here they have a different solution to the problem. Bear-poles are provided at shelters for hanging food-bags out of reach, about 15' high with a long, forked pole to hoist the bags to the top - quite a tricky procedure with a heavy food-bag!

We were up at 5.30am after a hot, restless night, and away at 6.35. The trail was easy and well-graded, but the weather was very hot and we stopped several times for water. Just after 1pm we arrived at Blackrock Hut (shelters are called "huts" in Shenandoah), in a lovely position in a deep valley with a good spring. A day hiker came down to fill his water bottles and stayed chatting with us for about an hour.

There were many gypsy moth caterpillars around and we noticed lots of trees stripped of their leaves. The damage seemed to be getting worse as we headed north and we often heard what sounded like rain, but it was the insect droppings pattering down as they ate the leaves.

Two other hikers arrived to stay the night. They were both experienced hikers and they each impressed us with some of their methods on the trail. One was Indiana Dan who was thru'-hiking north and does not carry a stove, but lights small fires with a steel and flint and cooks in a big metal basin rather like a wok. The other was a university lecturer who was heading south from Harpers Ferry to Springer Mountain in his 3 month vacation (having previously thru'-hiked the AT). He hoped to average 25 miles a day and his pack only weighed 16lbs. He achieved this by carrying no cooking equipment, just living on nuts, crackers, raisins, etc. Good luck to him.

Shortly after setting off next morning we met the day hiker who had visited us the previous afternoon. He had slept in his truck in a parking area and was hiking back to the shelter to see if we were fit to continue (we had told him about John's foot problem). Very thoughtful of him, he would have given us a lift off the Trail if we had been thinking of pulling out. But we were continuing, and it was an easy 6 miles to Loft Mountain campground where we stopped for more than an hour for a shower, laundry and resupply. As the AT shares the ridge with Skyline Drive through Shenandoah National Park there are many such facilities provided for the tourists, so we made use of all of them on our leisurely trek.

After doing our chores at the campground we went to the restaurant for a late breakfast, immediately followed by an early lunch! Then continued in hot weather to arrive at Pinefield Hut at 1pm. This was in another very pretty setting and we saw several deer grazing near the shelter. At about 3 o'clock the volunteer hutkeeper arrived and we chatted for about 2 hours. He then went back to his car and returned with an ice-box containing bread, cheese, ham, soup and cans of Coke. So we had a real feast with him. As we were finishing, three of his friends arrived and they all stayed until 7pm. We walked back up to the road with them and they insisted on giving us more "goodies" from their cars - cakes, crackers and some cherry flavoured tea-bags. A real gourmet day, and after all that company we had the shelter to ourselves for the night.

While we were eating our breakfast the next morning a deer was grazing nearby. She wandered off and soon returned closely followed by her fawn. We felt very privileged to have been trusted by this wild creature.

We were back on the trail by 7am for a short hike to Hightop Hut. It was warm and humid and we saw our first skunk ambling away up the hill beside the trail. Shortly after crossing the road at Simmons Gap we were hiking through the woods on the edge of a valley when Pam stopped and said "Did that rock move?" It did; it was a black bear! The first we had seen, it was about 50 yards ahead of us. As we opened the camera bag it was alerted by the sound of the Velcro fastener and ran off up the hillside, closely followed by another bear. We continued along the path and within 5 minutes saw another, much bigger, bear across the valley. It too ran off, but we had seen three bears, and it was still not 8am. What a day!

We arrived at Hightop Hut at 10.30am after hiking only 8.4 miles, but decided to stay there anyway as we had promised ourselves a leisurely time through Shenandoah. It was a hot day and after lunch we had an afternoon nap! Six other hikers arrived for the night and were very pleasant company.

Next day was again easy, hiking on the well graded trail and stopping at Lewis Mountain campground where we showered, laundered our clothes and bought groceries. We spent about 2 hours there and, after eating lunch, continued to Bearfence Mountain Hut. We arrived there at 2 o'clock and spent a quiet afternoon having hiked 12.5 miles. At about 7.30pm another hiker arrived and was good company. He was Ed "Bud Man" Seibert from Ohio and we were to enjoy his companionship on several occasions in the next few days.

As it got dark we noticed lots of fireflies twinkling in the undergrowth. We were awoken at about midnight by a thunderstorm and we lay watching the fireflies and the lightening - it was like a firework display.

We had planned to be up early and hike the 6 miles to Big Meadows Lodge for breakfast, but it was raining hard when we awoke at 5am, so we stayed in bed for another hour by which time the rain seemed to be easing. We were away by 6.40am and hiked through wet undergrowth and low cloud, but made good time. On our way we saw several deer with fawns and a woodchuck, which stood up on his hind legs to look around before seeing us and running away.

It was 1st July and at Big Meadows Lodge we completed 1000 miles on the Appalachian Trail. We were now only about 100 miles from Harpers Ferry, where we had started our hike 3 months ago, so we decided to continue and finish back at ATC Headquarters.

After a big buffet breakfast we telephoned our friend Chuck, who lives nearby, to let him know where we were and he offered to come and meet us on the following afternoon to take us home for the night. We then continued along the trail to Rock Spring Hut where we met the hutkeeper who was there doing some maintenance. The weather had brightened up and it was a warm and sunny afternoon. We were joined for the night by three lads who were out for 3 nights camping. It had rained for the first two nights in their tent so they had come to the shelter to dry out. Two of them were on their first camping trip and were not very impressed with being cold and damp!

We were up early and hiked 4.5 miles to Skyland for breakfast. We met Ed, who had been camping nearby, and we all went into the restaurant together. We were just finishing our meal when who should walk in but Chuck?!! He offered to "slack pack" us for the day, so we put our heavy gear in his truck and set off at 10.30am carrying just the essentials for a really enjoyable day's hike. The weather was perfect and we took time to stop and enjoy the beautiful views over the Shenandoah Valley. We took a short side trail to visit Mary's Rock which is a good viewpoint and is said to be more than a billion years old. Shortly after starting the descent from the rock we met Chuck who was hiking up the trail to meet us, so we hiked together down to Panorama, where we had a snack before being taken to his home for the night. His wife, Hazel, had prepared a lovely steak dinner and we celebrated our 1000 miles with a bottle of wine and a glass of brandy.

Next day Chuck offered to "slack pack" us again so he returned us to the Trail at Panorama. Within minutes of entering the woods we saw a bear a few yards away, it appeared to have been scavenging in the rubbish bins behind the restaurant. It was again bright and sunny as we hiked the 8.6 miles to Elkwallow Gap where we met Chuck at the cafe for lunch and then arranged to meet him later at a parking area on Skyline Drive to collect our packs before continuing the final 2 miles to the shelter. When he arrived he had two hikers and a dog in his truck and was going to run them to the local store and post office. He is a very generous person and will do anything to help hikers.

We really noticed the weight of our full packs after two days without them, and were glad that it was only 2 miles to Gravel Springs Hut. There was already an elderly couple there when we arrived; we learned that they were Carol (aged 73) and her husband Frank (who is deaf) who were hiking south along part of the AT, having already hiked a section of the Pacific Crest Trail earlier in the year.

We were up early next morning, but Carol and Frank were

already having breakfast and were on their way before us. This was to be our final day in Shenandoah National Park and we were planning to hike 10 miles to the next shelter. We had met lots of hikers in the Park, many of them passing us as they clocked up the miles, but we really enjoyed our leisurely trek.

When we arrived at the Tom Floyd Wayside shelter we found a message for us in the register. It was from Ed, inviting us to join him in Front Royal to celebrate Independence Day - it was 4th July. So after a quick lunch we set off again to head for town. We met some campers at a road crossing and they gave us drinks and apples and refilled our water bottles before we climbed over the final hill. By this time it was very hot as we walked along the highway and we stopped at a fruit stall to buy a melon and 12 nectarines which we ate before continuing. We had walked more than 2 miles along the road before a pick-up truck stopped and gave us a lift to the motel where Ed was staying. There didn't appear to be any fireworks or other public celebrations in town, so we went to a nice restaurant for a steak dinner. We were told that the temperature that day had been more than 90°F.

Next morning we went to a diner for breakfast and then got a lift back to the trail where we started hiking again at 10 o'clock. It was another very hot and humid day and we were glad that we had only planned a short hike to the next shelter. We climbed away from the road alongside the fence of the breeding centre of the National Zoological Park and were amused by the sign which reads:-

Pets on Leash
No Camping
No Fires
Stay on Trail
VIOLATORS
WILL BE EATEN

Having obeyed the rules we arrived safely at the Jim and Molly Denton shelter feeling very hot and sweaty. What a beautiful place it is, newly built with a picnic pavilion, porch and seats. And, the "pièce de résistance", a spring fed shower! This was wonderful, after the initial shock of the very cold water on our hot, sweaty bodies!

There was nobody at the shelter when we arrived, but we recognised Jeff's rucksack lying in the shelter with a note attached to say that he had gone to the nearby store. He had been following our progress in the registers since we returned to the AT and now that he had caught up with us he planned to slow down to our pace to stay with us until we came off the Trail. As we had enjoyed his company on many occasions since meeting him in Georgia we were really pleased for him to join us again for the final few days to Harpers Ferry.

Jeff soon returned and shortly afterwards Ed arrived so we all enjoyed a leisurely lunch together before Ed continued on his way. Several other hikers passed by during the afternoon, but we were pleased that we had decided to stay at this lovely shelter. We were particularly happy to be there in comfort when two violent thunderstorms brought torrential rain.

We were sorry to leave this wonderful place in the morning, but the Trail was calling and we were on our way shortly after 7am. It was cooler and fresher after yesterday's storms, but the undergrowth was very wet and the path was quite overgrown in places. We called at Manassas Gap shelter to fill our water bag at the spring as we had been warned that the water supply at the next shelter was not recommended. When we arrived at Dick's Dome shelter we were pleased that we had taken the trouble to carry water for 5 miles as the stream in front of the shelter was rather sluggish and uninviting. It was a very small shelter of a strange geodesic dome design and could only accommodate four people, so when other hikers arrived in the afternoon they put up their tents nearby.

Next morning we were away at 7.15am after just a cup of tea as we were heading to the Paris Restaurant only 5.5 miles away where the AT crosses US Highway 50. There we had a combined breakfast and lunch of eggs, steak and homefries (potatoes) which John and Jeff washed down with beer. (Yes, at 9.30 in the morning!) We left the restaurant some 2 hours later, having stocked up with cookies, crisps, chocolate and a few cans of Coke and beer, before hiking the 3.5 miles to Rod Hollow shelter.

The trail was again overgrown in places with several recent blowdowns. The weather was mild and overcast and we made good time to the shelter where we settled in for our now routine afternoon schedule of relaxing and drinking tea and, on this occasion, reading the Washington Post which we had bought at the restaurant. We also had the added enjoyment of the goodies we had bought earlier, which we shared with fellow hikers who arrived throughout the afternoon. There were ten of us at the shelter that night and as we had met most of the other hikers previously on the Trail we had a sociable time comparing notes of our experiences along the way.

Most of the other residents were up before us next morning, but we were really slowing our pace as we knew we only had a couple more days left on the Trail. The weather was again humid and the terrain had many ups and downs as we hiked the ten miles to Bears Den Youth Hostel (another excellent AYH). Along the way we saw a turkey cock which took off just a few feet in front of us; a most impressive sight as this big, powerful bird flew away through the trees.

We were greeted at the Hostel by the houseparents, John and Jenny, who gave us each a quart of lemonade and huge slices of watermelon before we settled in and showered. As John was about to go into the local town we accepted his offer of a lift and visited the supermarket where we bought steaks, sausages, salad and ice-cream. In the evening we made use of the hostel kitchen to cook a slap up meal.

After which we took a walk to see the view of the Shenandoah Valley from Bears Den Rocks before returning for a cup of coffee and more ice-cream.

We left the Hostel at 8.20am on another hot and humid day. Again there were many ups and downs as we hiked through the woods and entered West Virginia. We were only going eight miles to the Blackburn Trail Centre, run by the Potomac ATC, and we were again made really welcome by the caretakers, Jack and Jan. Sitting on the porch was Indiana Dan, a hiker we had previously met at the beginning of our hike through Shenandoah National Park. He had spent two days at the Hostel and was just about to continue on his way.

We were directed to a very pleasant bunkhouse above the garage, and shown the novel shower arrangements - an outdoor cubicle made of sacking with a large plastic bucket and spray nozzle suspended overhead. After filling the bucket with water you just stood underneath and turned on the nozzle. Lo-tech, but very effective on a hot day! Later we enjoyed an excellent dinner cooked by Jack and Jan and we spent a very sociable evening with several other hikers, most of whom we had met earlier on our hike.

The next day was 10th July and was to be our last day on the Appalachian Trail as it was only 12 miles to Harpers Ferry. John awoke with a hangover as a result of dehydration and the beer which had flowed freely the previous evening! He recovered somewhat after drinking six cups of water and several cups of tea, and we eventually got back on the trail. For the first time in several weeks he had no pain from his foot - just a severe headache!

It was another warm and humid day, but the gradients were easy as we hiked through the woods. We noticed lots of moths flying around, and learned that they were the gypsy moths which had just emerged to mate and lay their eggs. So we had seen their full life-cycle; egg clusters and chrysalises in Pennsylvania, caterpillars in Virginia and now the adult moths in West Virginia. And we had seen so many areas where the trees had been devastated by these tiny creatures.

We stopped at Keys Gap shelter where John rested while Pam went to the nearby store for some drinks and ice-cream then, suitably refreshed, we continued on the final stretch to Harpers Ferry. After the descent from Loudoun Heights we met Dave "Day Dreamer" and Maribeth walking across the bridge over the Shenandoah River. Dave was towing his rucksack on a luggage trolley which he had found abandoned under the bridge!

We all walked together to the headquarters building of the Appalachian Trail Conference, where we were greeted by Jean Cashin at the front desk. We had completed the southern half of the Appalachian Trail and had hiked 1103 miles through seven states. Of course we were very disappointed that we couldn't continue to complete the entire Trail, but we had really enjoyed our adventure and met wonderful people on the way.

Chapter 7

AFTER THE TRAIL : 1990/1991

It took us a long time to settle down to "real life" when we returned home from our hike in 1990. John went to see an orthopaedic surgeon to try to get treatment to cure the foot problem which had caused us to abandon our thru'-hike. He was told that nothing could be done and two year's rest from hiking was the only recommendation. After only two week's rest we were itching to get back on the Trail; but how? Alternative medicine? It was worth a try.

So a course of homeopathy was tried, but without much success. Acupuncture was suggested. It worked wonders. After only six 30-minute sessions over a period of two months the pain had gone and we were able to get back to the hills. We started with short walks and light packs, but soon were back in shape and carrying our full hiking kit. We felt confident that we could go back to America and hike the remaining 1050 miles of the Appalachian Trail.

We had to see if the foot would stand up to continuous hiking, so for 1991 we planned two long walks in Britain. In May we hiked out of our house near York and followed the Ebor Way to Ilkley, the Dales Way to the Lake District, the Coast to Coast to the North Yorks Moors, the Cleveland Way to Helmsley and the Ebor Way back home. A 270 mile circuit, through some of the most beautiful scenery in England. No problems; we completed the walk in less than three weeks.

Then in September we walked in Scotland from Braemar to Fort William, climbed Ben Nevis, then back via Aviemore and the Lairig Ghru to Braemar. Wonderful. We were ready to start planning a return to the United States in 1992.

Chapter 8

BACK ON THE TRAIL : 1992

Virginia : 1 April - 20 April.

In 1990 we had missed out 160 miles of the Trail in Virginia and a 17 mile section in Pennsylvania so we decided to fill in these gaps before starting the long trek north from Delaware Water Gap to Mount Katahdin in Maine.

On arrival in America we visited our friend Chuck Young who had again offered to take care of our spare boots, etc and mail them to us en route if required. So, having bought our first supply of groceries, Chuck drove us to Rockfish Gap where we would start hiking south to Catawba and thus complete the Virginia section of the AT. After having lunch at a restaurant at Rockfish Gap we said our goodbyes and once again set foot on the Appalachian Trail.

It was 1st April and quite humid with a light rain falling, but it was great to be back following the white blazes. We only hiked 5.3 miles, over Elk Mountain, to the Paul Wolfe Memorial shelter, a brand new shelter in a lovely situation beside Mill Creek. We found that we fell easily into the routine we had established in 1990, of collecting water and firewood, then making a cup of tea before unpacking our sleeping-bags, etc. We had been at the shelter for about an hour when two hikers arrived, but only stayed for about 20 minutes as they were aiming to get to Rockfish Gap for the night and it was already beginning to get dark. It was getting very cold so we had a quick snack and hot drink before getting to bed by 7 o'clock.

It was a cold night, but we slept well and awoke to a heavy

frost. After a breakfast of hot oats and two cups of tea we set off at 7.15am and immediately climbed 800' to the top of Dobie Mountain, so we didn't feel the cold! We soon descended to a parking area on the Blue Ridge Parkway (which the trail crosses several times) and then climbed 1200' up Humpback Mountain. There was a cold wind blowing when we stopped for lunch so we were quickly on our way again along the side of the ridge on a very rocky trail. We reached the Parkway again at Reeds Gap at 3.15pm after hiking 11.4 strenuous miles. By this time there was sleet in the air, so we decided to follow the road for 3 miles to spend the night at Rusty's Hard Time Hollow.

We had only gone a few hundred yards along the road when a Ranger stopped to see where we were heading. He warned us that this was the start of a belt of bad weather and advised us to get off the Trail and find shelter for a couple of days, so he gave us a lift to Rusty's. We had heard about this place when we were on the AT in 1990 and were determined to stay there. Rusty is an inventor who lives in an old homestead which he has renovated, but has no plumbing, electricity, gas or telephone. He is a most generous person and opens his home to hikers. We were made very welcome so we laid out our sleeping-bags in the bunkhouse before making ourselves comfortable in the cosy living room, heated by a wonderful wood-burning stove. There were three other hikers there and they cooked a good meal for us all in the evening.

Next morning there was a heavy frost, but no snow. After breakfast Rusty went out to his truck to listen to the weather forecast on the radio; this confirmed what the Ranger had told us. Rather than wait at Rusty's for the bad weather to pass, we accepted a lift to the town of Roanoke with two of the other hikers who had a vehicle and were planning to leave that day. From Roanoke we hired a car and went to visit friends in South Carolina for four days (our plan had been to visit them when we had completed our hike in Virginia, so we just brought it forward by a couple of weeks).

When we returned the hire car to Roanoke we heard that two feet of snow had fallen on the mountains over the past few days, so we had made the right decision. As we were now near the southern end of our Virginia hike, we planned to get back on the AT at Catawba and hike north to Rusty's and thus complete the section. So next day we returned to the store where we had reluctantly given up our attempt to "thru'-hike" and got a lift from there to the point where we had left the Trail.

It was wonderful to be back on the footbridge at Trout Creek where we had so sadly turned our back on the Appalachian Trail in 1990. We were soon back in the woods and the mountains, following the white blazes north. There were interesting rock formations along the top of the ridge and we followed the blue-blazed side trail to Dragon's Tooth, a spectacular rock monolith with good views, followed by a very steep and rocky descent. After descending to the valley we climbed up to Sawtooth Ridge which the trail follows for three miles, with fifteen ups and downs along the "teeth"! Then down again to the road where we got a lift to a motel for the night, having hiked 13 miles.

Next morning we got a lift back to the trail and immediately started climbing up the ridge on well graded switchbacks before following the ridge crest on a rocky trail. The weather was warm and sunny and we made good progress to McAfee Knob, a large slab of rock overhanging the valley, before a long descent to Brickey's Gap, where we had lunch. In the afternoon there was a long, tiring climb up Tinker Cliffs, followed by a good walk along the top before dropping down to Lambert's Meadow shelter. We arrived there at 3.20pm feeling hot and tired, but it had been a satisfying day with good views. We had hiked 10.2 miles and seen two turkeys, grouse, deer and a woodpecker.

We were back into the routine of shelter life, it all felt so familiar, as though we had never been away. Next morning we were on the trail by 7.20am and enjoyed a pleasant hike along Tinker Ridge,

Blue Ridge Mountains, NC
McAfee Knob, VA

with good views. We saw two wild goats which were very friendly! Although it had been cold at night the temperature soon rose and we had to stop several times for water. It was more than 80°F as we descended to Cloverdale, and there was no shade in the forest as the leaves were not yet on the trees.

The AT enters Cloverdale through the grounds of the Best Western motel, so we booked a room there for the night. It had happy memories for us as we had stayed there on our driving holiday in 1985. We arrived at 12.40pm and, after showering, walked to the supermarket to buy groceries and to the local Truck Stop to use the laundry. This was quite an expedition as Cloverdale is a big road intersection and we had to cross two highways and go under the Interstate, without the help of footpaths or bridges. All this "civilization" was quite a shock to the system, acres of concrete and hundreds of vehicles rushing by with all the associated noise and fumes. When we came out of the laundry it was raining hard so we went into a restaurant where we ate a big meal before returning to our room to write postcards and letters.

We got an early breakfast at the motel and were on our way at 7.15am. We again had to negotiate the road crossings, but the AT takes a roundabout route through woods and fields, and then over many stiles (which seemed to take us back and forth across the same fence!) as we paralleled the Interstate before passing under it on a small country road. After crossing the second highway and a railroad we finally started to climb away from all the noise and bustle and reached Fullhardt Knob shelter where we refilled our water bottles before continuing on a well graded trail in hot and sunny weather.

At Wilson Creek we met a group of volunteer trail-maintainers from Roanoke ATC so we stopped and chatted with them while we bathed our feet and refilled our water-bottles. We ate our lunch as they continued on their way up the trail, repainting blazes and cutting off overhanging branches. The whole Appalachian Trail is built and maintained by volunteers such as this from local hiking clubs affiliated to the Appalachian Trail Conference. They do a wonderful job and seem to be really happy in their work.

We reached Wilson Creek shelter after hiking 11.3 miles and again met the trail crew as they took a rest before continuing with their work. They had told us that the water supply was a long way down the mountainside, so we took both water bags and bottles to the stream and, while there we also washed ourselves and our socks, to save another journey. At about 4 o'clock there was a thunderstorm which freshened the air and reduced the temperature. After we got to bed that evening we were serenaded by a whippoorwill, but he did not continue into the night so we slept well. He woke us up at dawn though, so we had a leisurely breakfast before setting off for a short hike to Bobblets Gap shelter.

We arrived at the shelter at 11.25am after only hiking 7.5 miles but, as we had promised ourselves a meal at the excellent restaurant at Peaks of Otter the following day, we unpacked our gear and settled down for a restful afternoon. While we were eating our lunch a day-hiker arrived and stayed chatting with us for half an hour before continuing on his way. It was very hot and humid down in the little valley where the shelter is located and at 1.30pm we heard the first rumblings of thunder, which seemed to be all around us. After about 30 minutes the rain started, it was really torrential, but very refreshing after the sticky heat of the morning. Pam took advantage of it by taking a natural shower and hair wash! The sun was out again by 2.30pm - a natural hair dryer!

That night we had the company of thru'-hiker Mike "The Whaler" Petruniw from Connecticut. He had previously hiked the entire Appalachian Trail in 1990 so we spent a very interesting evening talking with him.

For 110 miles the Trail roughly parallels the Blue Ridge

Parkway. This scenic road was built during the Depression in the 1930s to give work to many unemployed. In places it was constructed over the route of the Appalachian Trail which then had to be relocated; so it now crosses back and forth across the Parkway from one side of the ridge to the other.

As we would be unable to reach Peaks of Otter in time for breakfast, we hiked along the trail in the morning before taking a detour on to the Parkway to visit the restaurant for lunch. We had hoped to take a room for the night at this beautiful lodge, but it was fully booked so after lunch we hiked for six miles along the road before returning to the trail. Shortly after reaching Cornelius Creek shelter The Whaler arrived and said that he was going to continue to the next shelter. So we joined him and hiked a further 4.6 miles over Apple Orchard Mountain to Thunder Hill shelter, making a total of 18.2 miles for the day, in lovely hiking weather - warm and sunny with a light breeze.

Two large rivers have cut through the ridge in this area, making gaps some 3000' deep. We had the long descent into the James River Gorge next morning and we made good time on a cool, overcast day arriving at Matts Creek shelter for lunch. We then continued to the highway beside the James River where we hitched a lift to the nearby town of Glasgow to resupply, arriving at about 4pm. Unfortunately the only motel had closed down, but a friendly motorist gave us a lift to a very smart hotel in the next town. We felt rather conspicuous in our hiking gear, but were made very welcome. A landscape architect with the U.S. Forest Service gave us a lift back to the Trail next day. We learned a lot from him about the local flora and fauna and about his work helping to maintain the James River Wilderness.

The climb up from the river was steep and rocky, but well graded and we made good time despite stopping several times to admire the views back across the gorge to the area we had hiked the previous day. We arrived at Punchbowl shelter at 3pm and began our usual routine, but this was disrupted when our new MSR Waterworks pump failed after pumping only two litres of water. John dismantled it and cleaned the filters, but to no avail so we lit a fire to boil water for cooking and drinking. The shelter is situated next to a lovely pond, but this seemed less idyllic when the peepers and bullfrogs started their chorus which continued through the night.

We didn't awake until 6.40am so we started hiking later than usual, but it was only nine miles to the next shelter and the terrain was easy with no major climbs. Spring had arrived with warm, sunny weather; the leaves were appearing on the trees and spring flowers bloomed beside the trail attracting masses of butterflies. We met a group of trail maintainers from the Natural Bridge ATC, who were obviously enjoying being out on the trail on this beautiful day.

After crossing the Pedlar River on a footbridge just below the Pedler Dam we climbed the ridge and followed the edge of the lake, some 500' above the shore, crossing many streams flowing down into the lake. The trail then followed Brown Mountain Creek upstream for a mile to the shelter. It was a beautiful walk beside the tumbling stream and the Brown Mountain Creek shelter is set up above it amongst pine trees. A lovely place to stay on a warm spring afternoon with butterflies fluttering around.

Next day we continued the gentle climb up to the head of the creek before ascending steeply on switchbacks through the forest, passing three other hikers, on the way to the summit of Bald Knob (4,059'). It was Good Friday and we arrived at Cow Camp Gap shelter by lunchtime, but decided to stay for the night as it was ten miles to the next shelter and we thought that it may be full with weekend hikers by the time we would get there. We spent a relaxing afternoon, chatting with several hikers who stopped for a rest then continued on their way.

Three hikers joined us for the night. They were John

"Greybeard" Whiting from Michigan who is hiking the AT in sections over several years; and George Boss and Bob Rascoe, a furniture manufacturer from Virginia and a lawyer from North Carolina, who were only out for the three days of the Easter holiday. As they were on a short hike they were carrying "real" food with them. As well as sharing their steaks with us, they also handed round the Scotch, bourbon and white wine with the meal! They were great company and we spent a very sociable evening.

We were up at 6am after a reasonable night's sleep, despite two snorers in the shelter! It was dull and hazy as we hiked up Cold Mountain (4,022'), but there were good views from the top. Soon the sun came out and we had an enjoyable morning hiking along the ridge with many extensive views. We arrived at Seeley-Woodworth shelter just after noon and had time for a good wash before being joined by John, George and Bob - last night's companions. Another great time was had by all; this time Virginia country ham was on the menu!

Easter Sunday dawned damp and misty, but we were away by 7am as we had a long day ahead. We came out above the cloud on The Priest (4,063') and then descended 3,100' to the Tye River, which we crossed on a swinging suspension bridge. It was warm and sunny in the valley so we stopped for lunch on the rocks beside the river before climbing up the far side. We spent the night at Harpers Creek shelter in a lovely high valley beside a tumbling stream. No-one else came to the shelter so we spent a quiet evening watching a pair of nuthatches nesting in the tree outside.

We awoke to thick fog and as we climbed up the Three Ridges we got deeper into cloud and rain, so we saw none of the views mentioned in the guide-book. While we were having lunch at Maupin Field shelter the sun tried to break through the cloud, without much success. But there wasn't far to go now and we reached Rusty's Hard Time Hollow at 12.30pm to complete our hike of the 160 miles in

Virginia. Rusty greeted us like long lost friends and then took us to the bus station at Charlottesville.

After a short visit to our friend, Chuck, we travelled by bus to Harrisburg, Pennsylvania to visit the friends we had made in 1990. Jon and Diane had put us up at their home during a heavy snowfall and we were now back to spend a few days with them and to hike 17 miles of the Trail we had missed during the storm.

On 28th April Diane drove us to the AT crossing of US Highway 11 and we hiked the 17.6 miles north to Duncannon. It was a fine, sunny day and, with light packs, we averaged 3 m.p.h. for the first half of the hike on the newly relocated trail in the Cumberland Valley. It was very pleasant walking beside Conodoguinet Creek through masses of bluebells, and across grassy fields. Then we climbed up Cove Mountain and the rest of the route was rough and rocky, just as we remembered Pennsylvania from our previous hike. We stopped at Hawk Rock to admire the superb view of the town of Duncannon and the Susquehanna River, before tackling the steep, rocky descent. We were met at Duncannon by Diane who took us back to their home, where she had prepared a splendid meal to celebrate John's birthday.

So we had filled in the gaps and completed the 1,268 miles of the Appalachian Trail from Springer Mountain in Georgia to the Pennsylvania/New Jersey border. Now we would travel to Delaware Water Gap to begin the remaining 878 miles to Mount Katahdin.

New Jersey and New York : 29 April - 13 May.

On 29th April Jon and Diane drove us to Delaware Water Gap where we began the trek north towards Mount Katahdin in Maine. We hiked across the bridge which carries the interstate highway over the Delaware River in to New Jersey. The trail headed off into the woods

Pennsylvania Rocks
Sunfish Pond, NJ

climbing up beside Dunnfield Creek to the top of the ridge. It was hot and sunny, and we met several day-hikers on our way to Sunfish Pond - a beautiful glacial lake which the trail skirts on rocks. Camping is not allowed near the pond so we continued until we found an area where we could pitch our tent, with good views to both sides of Kittatinny Ridge.

We awoke to a cold morning so, after a breakfast of tea and hot oats, we quickly packed the tent and were on our way by 7.20am. The trail continued along the ridge, at times on old roads, but often it was rough and rocky with some short, steep climbs and scrambles, reminiscent of the conditions in Pennsylvania. Light rain started around noon, but we continued to Brink Road shelter, arriving at 3 o'clock having hiked 15.5 miles. The rain had stopped, but it became quite cold in the evening so we were in bed at 7pm, only to be awoken an hour later by the piercing call of a whippoorwill! Fortunately he didn't stay too long and we were soon asleep again.

We were awake at 5.30am and on the trail by 6.45 on a beautiful sunny morning. When we reached the road at Culvers Gap we visited Worthington's Bakery for coffee and cinnamon buns. There are many road crossings in New Jersey so we often took short detours for a meal at a diner to supplement our camp food. It is estimated that a hiker can burn up to 5,000 calories a day, and there is no way we can carry enough food to supply this need. So we both lost weight - John 40lbs and Pam 16lbs.

After our break at Culvers Gap we walked through woods with forsythia in bloom and soon climbed back up to the ridge crest with good views through the trees of lakes on either side of the ridge. After another short climb we reached the summit of Sunrise Mountain (1,653'), and were surprised to find a big stone shelter and a car park there. There were two large motorcycles in the car park and we chatted for a while with a couple on one of them. We expressed our surprise at finding that a road came to the top of the mountain, and they were surprised that anyone should consider walking to the top! Before leaving they filled our water bottles from a flask of water they were carrying and we continued on our way on a very undulating trail.

After stopping for lunch at Mashipacong shelter we met a southbound hiker "Bog Scouter" who had set out from Massachusetts and was heading for Georgia, then he would travel back to Mass. and hike north to Mount Katahdin to complete the AT.

At 3pm we followed the steep, rocky side trail to Rutherford shelter, having hiked 16 miles. We found a bird's nest built inside the shelter, so we set up our bedding at the opposite end. There were three pinkish eggs in the nest and, after we were in bed, the bird returned and sat on the nest. Next morning there were four eggs. We later learned that the bird was a phoebe, and we were to share shelters with several of them during our hike.

Next morning we continued hiking along the Kittatinny Ridge through High Point Monument State Park in lovely sunny weather. After passing close to the monument (at 1803' the highest point in New Jersey) we descended the ridge and then found ourselves walking through fields and crossing many streams and boggy areas. We crossed Vernie Swamp on 111 bog bridges - we counted them!

We walked along the road to the small town of Unionville (across the border in New York state), where we planned to stay in a hostel at the Inn. We knew that the Inn was closed and for sale, but we had been told that the hostel was still available for hikers. As we walked into town a young man in a pick-up truck slowed down and started talking to us. He was very interested in what we were doing and invited us to stay at his house as he said that the hostel was no longer open. We decided to find out for ourselves and, when we could find no one at the Inn, we found his house and accepted his very generous offer. He was Robert Mally, who invited us in and introduced us to his wife, Rosie.

They made us very welcome in their home and invited friends round to meet us. We bought some steaks at the local store and, in the evening, Robert cooked them and served them with salad and potatoes. An excellent meal and good company. Shortly after getting into our sleeping bags for the night a violent thunderstorm started, making us feel very grateful to be inside.

We were awake early as Rosie had to be up at 4.30am to attend a horse show where she was competing. Robert cooked bacon and eggs for breakfast and we left Unionville at 6.45am with very happy memories of a pleasant evening with very generous people.

We were soon out of town and stayed at low level, crossing fields in the Wallkill Valley. After crossing the bridge over the Wallkill River we followed the trail on a dirt road for 1.5 miles round three sides of a sod farm (a huge flat field in the valley bottom where they grow turf). After nearly 5 miles of walking in this flat valley we were glad to turn off into the woods to start the climb up Pochuck Mountain. We stopped for a break at the new Pochuck Mountain shelter, then continued over two ridges before reaching the main summit, with good views back to High Point and the Kittatinny Ridge. Then down again and through more swampy areas before we took the road into the tiny hamlet of Glenwood, New Jersey.

It was here that we experienced our bit of "Trail Magic". A few days earlier Pam had a dental bridge come loose, so we needed to find a dentist. We had planned to treat ourselves to bed and breakfast at the Apple Valley Inn in Glenwood and we arrived there just after lunch on a Sunday. After settling in and showering, we asked the owners, John and Mitzi Durham, where the nearest dentist was as we would have to visit him tomorrow. We were told "There's one working out in the yard"!! Sure enough, a young dentist was lodging there while he looked for a house to buy in the area, and at weekends he helped out with the gardening. So we went and told him our problem and he offered to look at it. When he had finished his chores he took us about ten miles to his surgery where he fixed the tooth, then drove us back to the Inn - all on a Sunday afternoon.

So we were back on the trail on Monday morning without losing a day. Initially the trail followed roads out of Glenwood, but soon we crossed a stile into fields, many of them low-lying with lots of bog bridges. After entering woods we began the 1000' climb of Wawayanda Mountain on a very rocky trail, but well graded with switchbacks and rock steps. At the top we stopped for a drink and to look at the views before beginning the gradual descent of the mountain. We continued past the sign to Wawayanda shelter to visit the headquarters of Wawayanda State Park, where we filled our water bottles and bags from the hose in the maintenance yard. While there we chatted with a Park Ranger and were invited inside for coffee. We sat for about forty minutes talking to the Maintenance Superintendent before we walked back along the trail to the new shelter which was in a very nice position in the woods.

It rained heavily during the night and there was still light rain falling when we left at 7.15am. The first 4 miles were through woods, crossing several streams, but after crossing the state-line into New York we were following the top of the ridge on sloping, lichen covered rocks which were wet and slippery in the rain; and we were unable to see the views in the poor visibility. As we descended the ridge to cross US Highway 17A the weather showed no signs of improving, so we decided to follow the road to the village of Greenwood Lake, from where we phoned John Durham and arranged to spend another night at Apple Valley Inn. He agreed to pick us up at a diner on his way home from work and we returned for another pleasant night at Glenwood, where our host offered to "slack pack" us the next day. So he returned us to the trail in the morning and we hiked 13.8 miles with light packs.

It was a cool and sunny day and we hiked the first five miles in

2 hours, mostly on woodland paths, but with some rocky scrambles. We crossed the stream at the base of beautiful Fitzgerald Falls and then climbed the steep rock steps at the side of the waterfall to regain the top of the ridge. From Mombasha High Point (1,280') there were excellent views and we could see the skyline of Manhattan on the horizon, some forty miles away. After a very steep scramble down to US Highway 17 we followed the road to a small grocery store where John had arranged to meet us, so we sat outside at a picnic table eating snacks and drinking coffee before returning once again to Glenwood.

Next morning we were returned to the Trail early, and were hiking by 7am. It was frosty at first, but the sun soon came out for a very pleasant cool, sunny day. Our route took us through Harriman State Park with many ups and downs on an ungraded trail. After walking through woods and passing several swamps we came to the Lemon Squeezer, an interesting scramble up through a steep cleft in the rocks - our big packs only just scraped through! In this section we were passing through an old iron mining area, with remains of some of the pits still visible. During the Civil War this was a thriving industrial area with the iron ore being mined and smelted locally before being transported to West Point to be made into guns and shells.

After passing over Fingerboard Mountain (1,328') we took a detour along the road to Lake Tiorati to collect water, as we had been warned that the supply at the next shelter was of doubtful quality. At the lake we found a tourist area with a Ranger station and Coke machine so we stopped there for our lunch break. We chatted with the Ranger, and he filled our water bags from his own supply. It was a short walk up through the woods to the William Brien Memorial shelter, which is built of stone under a rocky outcrop. We spent the afternoon sunbathing on large rocks in front of the shelter and writing postcards. A southbound hiker stopped to eat his lunch and then continued on his way.

We were awake at 5.30am and on our way by 6.30 in light

showery rain, but we still had good views of the Hudson River, and again saw New York City on the horizon. After descending from Black Mountain we had to cross Palisades Interstate Parkway, which we managed to reach in the rush hour, with streams of cars rushing towards New York. We successfully negotiated this brush with civilization and were glad to get back into the woods, where we stopped at Beechy Bottom Brook to refill our water bottles, before tackling the long climb up West Mountain. There were good views to both sides from the ridge crest before we descended, crossing several old woods roads which are now waymarked as cross country ski trails. It was an easy climb up Bear Mountain, which has a tourist road to the stone observation tower at the top, and good views as we started the descent to the Hudson River valley.

At the end of the long descent we were hiking through civilization, passing a ski jump before reaching a public park and the Bear Mountain Inn. We treated ourselves to an excellent lunch at the Inn before continuing on our way, hiking through the grounds of a zoo before crossing the Hudson River on the busy Bear Mountain suspension bridge; it is only an hour's drive from New York City and at 124' is the lowest point on the Appalachian Trail. We were glad to get back into the woods and leave the noise of traffic behind.

As we climbed up Anthony's Nose from the river it started to rain, and continued as we hiked through the woods along the ridge, stopping at a view point to look down on the Hudson, with the Bear Mountain Bridge to the left and West Point Military Academy to the right. We descended the ridge on an easy trail, at times using old carriage roads, before crossing a swampy area on bog bridges to reach US Highway 9. After crossing the road, and another swamp, we climbed up the hill to reach the Old West Point Road. From here we turned right to reach Graymoor Monastery, another establishment on the Appalachian Trail where hikers are welcome to spend the night. We were greeted by Father Cuthbert who showed us to our rooms - individual monks cells, simply furnished with bed, desk and wash basin. Hot showers were available and we were offered the use of a washing-machine and dryer. Promptly at 5.30pm Brother Gerry escorted us to the dining-room where a wonderful spread awaited us - soup, salad, pasta with lobster and a delicious selection of desserts. As much as we could eat. It was really interesting to talk to the friars and learn about their work, and they seemed to be equally interested in what we were doing.

Next morning another vast spread was laid out in the dining-room - fresh fruit, cereals, muffins, fruit juice, French toast with bacon, tea and coffee. Those monks really know that the way to a hiker's heart is through his stomach!

There had been heavy rain during the night so it was wet and misty in the woods, but soon the sun came out and the undergrowth began to dry. We followed the undulating trail over several small hills, but there were no serious climbs so we made good time. There are no shelters on this section of trail, so we headed for Fahnestock State Park where we put up our tent at the campground although it wasn't officially open and we were the only campers there.

Next morning we bushwhacked up the ridge, rather than retracing our steps for a mile along the road, and were happy to find the trail without too much trouble. We had a short break at a spot with a lovely view down to Canopus Lake then continued the easy climb to the summit of Shenandoah Mountain (1,282') before the long, gradual descent to reach Ralph's Peak Hikers Cabin. We met the caretaker, Joe Hrouda, there and chatted with him while we had a drink and snack. He told us that he didn't recommend the campsite we were heading for as it was close to the interstate highway so we decided to continue beyond it to the next shelter. As we arrived at the side trail to the campsite at 11.30am this extra mileage was no great hardship!

As we were approaching NY Highway 52 we were surprised to

find a bright orange warning sign erected on the trail - "Caution Road Work 100ft"! Sure enough, when we arrived at the road crossing there were extensive road works in progress, so the sign was justified although it seemed rather out of place on a hiking trail.

We took a short detour along the road to Mountain Top Store where we had a superb chicken sandwich and fresh fruit salad for lunch, then returned to the trail for an easy 3.5 miles to the Morgan Stewart shelter. We had been there about one hour when another hiker, Larry, arrived. He was a chef from New York City out for a week's hike to escape from the rat race and was very good company.

Next day we hiked only five miles to the village of Poughquag where we were to take a day off to do the chores. We arrived at the village store/deli at 9am, so stopped there for breakfast before continuing to the Pine Grove Motel where we had booked a room. After unpacking and showering we were driven to the supermarket by Mr Patel, the owner of the motel, and then had a leisurely walk back via the bank and a coffee shop. We were offered the use of a washing machine and drier at the motel, so we did the laundry in the afternoon, and later we were given a share of the Patels' delicious curry for our supper.

We were given a ride back to the trail next morning and started hiking before 7am. It was already sunny, and by midday the temperature had risen to 80°F. In the morning we climbed over dry, rocky ridges with low lying swampy areas between. These we crossed on wooden walkways or bog bridges which had been built to protect the fragile ecosystem from us - and us from it! We crossed the railroad at the new Appalachian Trail station, which has been built to provide a weekend train service for hikers out of New York City. After taking photographs of this unique little halt, we turned on to the road and walked half a mile to Tony's Deli where we had roast beef sandwiches and drinks before returning to the trail.

For the next 2.7 miles we hiked through the Pawling Nature Preserve where there were many overgrown, boggy areas - often with no bog bridges or logs to walk on. We then emerged on to a grassy road and passed the ornamental iron gates of the "Gate of Heaven Cemetery" which seemed rather out of place, but the area had obviously once been well populated and farmed as we passed the remains of many old stone walls.

We were hot and tired when we arrived at the Webatuck shelter after hiking 14 miles on a very hot day so, after pumping water, we had a restful afternoon. The shelter looked quite old, but was very neat and clean and was well equipped with a coffee pot and frying pan hanging on the wall, as well as a broom and shovel. We were visited by the shelter caretaker in the evening, who gave us quite a shock when he arrived as he was wearing military type clothing and carried a machete and two-way radio on his belt. He stayed and chatted for about an hour and told us that the machete was to protect himself from rabid animals! He told us that the shelter was built in 1940, but he does his best to keep it in good condition and provides all the little extras for the hikers. He seemed very conscientious and said that he tries to visit the shelter every day after work.

Next morning we crossed into the state of Connecticut after hiking just over a mile from the shelter. It was 13th May and we had hiked 164 miles through the states of New Jersey and New York in the past two weeks. We had been very close to the most highly populated areas of the United States and, at times, had seen and heard signs of civilization. We had taken advantage of nearby stores and restaurants, but most of the time the trail had felt completely remote from the modern world.

Connecticut and Massachusetts : 13 May - 25 May.

The Appalachian Trail meanders for 50 miles through the northwestern corner of Connecticut and another 88 miles through the Berkshire Hills in western Massachusetts, following the Housatonic River for most of the route. We crossed the Ten Mile River on the Ned Anderson Memorial Bridge at the point where that river flows into the Housatonic and then followed the river bank to Bull's Bridge. Here we took a detour over the old covered bridge to the Country Mart for a late breakfast.

When we returned to the trail we also returned briefly to New York State as our route followed the road for 2.6 miles before climbing through the woods up the shoulder of Schaghticoke Mountain. In this area the trail passes through the Schaghticoke Indian Reservation and along the ridge there were good views from Indian Rocks, before we clambered through rocky ravines with names like Dry Gulch and Rattlesnake Den.

After descending to cross Thayer Brook we climbed over Mount Algo to reach the shelter at 1.30pm after hiking 12.5 miles. Mount Algo shelter is situated on a beautiful wooded hillside with a lovely stream flowing past, just right for a refreshing bathe before lunch on a hot and humid day. This is one of a series of new shelters built by the Appalachian Mountain Club in Connecticut, beautifully constructed from cedar and pine logs. Campfires are not permitted at these shelters so we had to use our stove for all our cooking. This should have been no problem, but our water filter failed at the first shelter so we had to boil all our drinking water. Consequently our supply of Coleman fuel didn't last long and we had to take an unplanned trip off the trail to buy more. We also managed to get a new filter for the pump, but it continued to give intermittent trouble.

We left Mount Algo shelter at 7am for the 30 minute walk to

the village of Kent, where we had breakfast at The Villager Restaurant, before making use of the laundromat, post office and grocery store. We had also planned to buy some replacement equipment at the backpacking store, but arrived there to find a notice on the door saying that it was only open on Saturday and Sunday. As this was Thursday we had to give it a miss and were fortunate to find that the hardware store stocked Coleman fuel, but only in gallon cans; so we bought one, filled our fuel bottles and left the rest to be given to any other hikers who followed.

After doing all our chores we were back on the trail at 9.45am and climbed up to Caleb's Peak (1,160') with good views back over Kent and the Housatonic Valley. It was a pleasant sunny day with a gentle breeze, and the trees now had sufficient leaves to give some shade. The trail descended steeply off the Peak on some good switchbacks and rock steps, before climbing again through the forest. This brought us to St. John's Ledges, the top of a steep granite cliff, much enjoyed by rock climbers. Mere hikers do not feel so comfortable here though and the very steep 500' descent has only been made possible by a series of rock steps.

On reaching the bottom of the cliff the trail followed a dirt road alongside the river for a very easy and pleasant walk to Stewart Hollow Brook shelter. We passed through a beautiful plantation of red pines which were planted in the 1930s, but they are not native to Connecticut and are now dying so some of the logs have been used to build the new AT shelters.

We continued along the road beside the river for 2.6 miles the next morning, before the first of several stiff climbs along the crest of the ridge. It was a hot, sunny day and we soaked our steaming feet in a stream while we ate our lunch. We then continued to Pine Swamp Brook shelter where we arrived at 12.10pm after hiking 10.4 miles with 2,500' of climbs.

It rained through the night, but had stopped by the time we left the shelter. It was a pleasant walk through the damp, cool woods along the ridge crest with some good views. At one point we passed a large wooden platform used for launching hang gliders, and looked down on to the Lime Rock Race Track which is used for testing brakes for the motor manufacturers. These modern facilities seemed a world away from our simple existence on the Appalachian Trail, and we were pleased that all was quiet as we passed by.

When we reached US Highway 7 we walked along the road to The Village Coffee Shop and Restaurant, a very friendly establishment where we were served an excellent breakfast and signed their hikers' register. We also telephoned our friend Ann Cuddy, a lady we had met back in the Smokies during our 1990 hike. She had said we were to call her when we were in her area so, rather belatedly, we did and were invited to visit her home for the night. She arranged to pick us up at the Iron Bridge over the Housatonic River at Falls Village, so we returned to the trail and hiked two miles through beautiful pine woods along the river.

We arrived at the bridge much earlier than expected so we went into the village to find a coffee shop. When we asked to be directed to one we set off along the road and, after walking for about 10 minutes, we realised that we were heading for the place where we had had breakfast! So we retraced our steps to the village centre and asked at The Inn, a very smart place, if they served coffee. They were not yet open for the day but we said that we would sit out on the porch and, not only did they provide us with coffee, they would take no payment - it was "on the house".

When we returned to the river we watched canoeists practising in the rapids below the power station outlet until Ann arrived to drive us to her lovely home at Lakeville. After lunch we were taken to town to buy groceries and also spares for our water pump, then returned for a very pleasant evening and good meal.

Next day was cool and overcast as we set off with heavy packs after our resupply. At the Iron Bridge the trail leaves the Housatonic River to climb over the ridge, but we were to meet the river again later. The area near Salisbury is very popular with local walkers and we met several as we hiked over Barrack Matiff and descended steeply to the road, which we followed past Salisbury before climbing up the ridge on the other side of the valley. We climbed steeply to the summit of Lion's Head (1,738'), with good views, before descending to the Riga shelter. This beautiful new shelter is situated on the edge of the ridge with extensive views eastwards across the valley to Twin Lakes. This was the first shelter we had visited which had a view, all the others had been in the woods. We looked forward to seeing a spectacular sunrise from our beds, but we awoke to a misty morning with only a hazy sun managing to penetrate the grey.

The day's hike started with a long climb to the summit of Bear Mountain (2,316') with good views from the rocky ledges, before descending steeply on a rocky trail into Sages Ravine, a beautiful area with big pine trees and tumbling waterfalls. In the ravine we passed the sign welcoming us to the state of Massachusetts and began the long, gradual ascent of Race Mountain (2,365'), followed by a descent of 500' before climbing to the summit of Mount Everett (2,602') on slippery rocks and roots. By now it was raining and we had climbed up into the cloud, so we saw none of the views, but after arriving at Glen Brook shelter the rain stopped and we were able to dry our clothes.

Next day was clear and bright so we could look back at Mount Everett and forwards to Mount Greylock, at 3,491' the highest point in Massachusetts and some five days hiking away. After the steep descent off Jug End there was a rather boring, flat road-walk across the Housatonic Valley before climbing the ridge and following the 3 mile roller-coaster of East Mountain. We saw our only poisonous snake on

Riga shelter, CT
Campfire at Stratton Pond, VT

this section, a copperhead which was stretched across the trail. John tried to move it away with a stick but it got quite aggressive and started striking at the stick, so we took a detour over some rocky ledges and left it in peace to enjoy it's sunbathing!

We arrived at the luxurious Tom Leonard shelter at 1.35pm after hiking 13.3 miles. The shelter has built-in wooden bunks and a sleeping loft, but has a very long climb down to the spring! Later in the afternoon we were joined by a father and son, John and Chris Woodall, from South Carolina who had been hiking the Appalachian Trail in sections over a six year period and would complete the entire Trail in a few more weeks. They had been following our progress in the registers all the way from New Jersey.

Our companions were up and away before us in the morning, but we were on the Trail by 7 o'clock. It was a chilly morning and it felt particularly cold as we descended from the shelter to scramble through rough and rocky Ice Gulch, but then the footing was easier as we hiked through woodland. At Benedict Pond there is a swimming area with a sandy beach, but we just admired the beautiful setting before climbing to The Ledges with good views back to Mount Everett. We arrived at the side trail to Mount Willcox North shelter, where we had planned to spend the night, at 10.30am so we decided to continue to the village of Tyringham. We descended steadily, passing several swampy areas and old beaver ponds; and then hiked through Beartown State Forest, where the trail seemed to have been recently relocated, before reaching the ridge overlooking the Tyringham Valley.

The Appalachian Trail used to pass through Tyringham, but it has been relocated so we took the old route into the village where we were directed to the home of Carolyn Cannon who provides lodging for hikers. She allowed us to use her washing machine and then took us for a drive to a farm to buy some fresh milk. On the way she took us on a guided tour of the village pointing out the house where she was born nearly eighty years ago and relating much local gossip!

We let ourselves out of Miss Cannon's house at 6.50am, but we thought someone was up before us when we heard a hammering noise as we walked through the village. We soon saw the source of the noise though, not a keen handyman already at work, but a woodpecker tapping away at the plastic downpipe on a house!

It was a cool morning, but we soon warmed up as we climbed out of the village. As we hiked along the ridge we could see Upper Goose Pond through the trees, but we did not take the side trail to the cabin beside the pond preferring to remain on the trail which soon descended to cross the Massachusetts Turnpike on a bridge built for the AT. Shortly afterwards we reached and crossed US Highway 20 before climbing to reach the summit of Becket Mountain (2,180'), followed by Walling Mountain (2,220') then down a rocky trail to Finerty Pond where we had our lunch. It was a very pretty spot, but there were a lot of flies about so we were quickly on our way and climbed over Bald Top Mountain (2,040') before reaching October Mountain shelter at 2pm. When we arrived at the shelter we noticed that the edges of the picnic-table/bench and the front of the shelter had been badly gnawed. Looking around we found what we assumed to be porcupine quills on the ground. We had the company of another hiker, Sam from Connecticut, for the night. He confirmed that the damage to the shelter was indeed caused by porcupines, so we carefully hung all our equipment from the roof as we had heard stories of boots and rucksack harnesses being eaten by porkies in their constant craving for salt.

Sure enough, we had our first encounter with porkies that night. We were awoken at about 9.30pm by rustling and gnawing noises and shone the torch outside to see a porcupine gnawing at the picnic table. We shooed him away, but were awoken again before midnight - this time there were two of them out there! After watching them for a while we again shooed them away and we eventually got back to sleep.

The next day was very hot and we were glad of the shade of the trees as we hiked through the woods on a rough trail with many roots and rocks. We again descended into the Housatonic Valley to cross the river for a final time, having followed it closely for the last 108 miles. Once off the ridge the trail follows a road for 2.6 miles through the edge of the town of Dalton, where we took a detour to a motel and were glad to get into our air-conditioned room - the temperature outside was 96°F. We had two days off in Dalton; buying groceries, doing laundry, writing letters and getting haircuts. We met Kay Wood, a member of the local branch of the Appalachian Mountain Club (AMC), and she offered to "slack-pack" us up Mount Greylock (i.e. she took our heavy packs in her car while we hiked to the summit).

So next morning we left most of our equipment at the motel, to be collected later by Kay, and we set off just before 6am carrying only the essentials for a day-hike. It was great to be free of our 40lb packs and we had a most enjoyable day. We climbed over several forested ridges before coming down to the Hoosic River in the small town of Cheshire, where we stopped at the store for a second breakfast at 9am. The Appalachian Trail goes along the main street in Cheshire, but it was very quiet when we passed through on a Sunday morning. After following the road out of town we soon came to the sign directing us across a field and up a steep hillside. The trail then climbed steadily through forest for more than five miles to the 3,491' summit of Mount Greylock. We were in cloud for the final four miles, so we did not see any views, but we had enjoyed our hike and arrived at Bascom Lodge on the summit at 1.15pm. We checked in for a night stop at the Lodge, a superb establishment run by the AMC providing lodging, showers, meals and a shop for hikers - and others, as there is a road to the top!

We had a light lunch at the snack bar and were soon joined by Sam, who had been with us at October Mountain shelter. He continued on his way, but we relaxed in the porch and chatted with an AMC naturalist until Kay Wood arrived with our rucksacks. So we could then shower and change into fresh clothes before being served an excellent meal. We spent a very sociable evening by the big log-fire chatting with Kay - she is 74 years old and hiked the AT at age 70. She is still a very active hiker and trail-maintainer, a wonderful recommendation for healthy exercise and the outdoor life.

When we awoke next morning the sky was clear and blue, with extensive views; but the trees were white with frost, and the ice showered down on us as we descended through the forest. It was a long way down to the valley where we crossed the road, railroad and the Hoosic River before beginning the very pleasant climb up the other side beside Sherman Brook. After about two miles we left the brook and the trail became steeper, with a stiff rock scramble to the top of the ridge where we crossed the state line into Vermont.

Vermont : 25 May - 8 June.

The Appalachian Trail heads north for 100 miles through the Green Mountains of Vermont before turning eastwards to pass over lower hills for another 44 miles to cross the Connecticut River into New Hampshire.

So far we had had most shelters to ourselves, but we arrived in Vermont on Memorial Day, which is the start of the summer holiday season in America, so we began to see more and more people on the Trail. We had a pleasant walk through the woods along the top of the ridge and saw the first lady's slipper orchids and azaleas in bloom. We also saw a porcupine foraging on the forest floor, but when it heard us it very rapidly climbed up a tree. We were surprised that it was so agile.

We arrived at the Seth Warner shelter at 2pm having hiked 13.5 miles. After a beautiful sunny morning the weather turned cool and cloudy in the afternoon and there were a lot of flies about, so we lit a fire. After dinner it got quite cold and we got into our sleeping bags early, but at 7.30 another hiker arrived so we got up and rearranged our gear to make room for him. His name was Ed Caco and he was on his first day on The Long Trail, which begins at the Massachusetts/Vermont stateline and uses the same footway as the AT for 100 miles, before continuing north through Vermont for a total of 265 miles to the Canadian border.

We awoke to a cold morning, but it was pleasant hiking weather as we set off over many ridges and peaks of the Green Mountains. We passed a beaver pond with a huge dam, quite an amazing piece of engineering which was holding back a vast quantity of water. From here northwards we were to see evidence of much beaver activity and never failed to marvel at their work. On two occasions the trail actually crossed beaver dams, which was a worrying prospect at first but once on them we found them to be very strong and safe structures.

After a very steep 1,000' descent to Highway 9 we had an equally long climb up the other side to reach the Melville Neuheim shelter at 2.20pm where Ed later joined us. It was nice to have company and we got to know him quite well in the following week as we met up each night.

We awoke to another cold morning, but once we were on the trail it was fine weather for hiking with a clear blue sky and good visibility. There were good views of Little Pond and Glastonbury Mountain and, when we stopped for a break at Goddard shelter, the view back to Mount Greylock was quite spectacular. After climbing over Glastonbury Mountain (3,748') it started raining so we were unable to light a fire when we reached Kid Gore shelter. As the water pump was again giving trouble we boiled plenty of water on the stove. After three hot drinks to warm us up Pam got into her sleeping-bag to keep warm and discovered that the Nalgene bottles filled with boiled water made excellent hot water bottles for warming feet! Ed arrived at 5.20pm, very tired, cold and wet having hiked all afternoon in the rain. After cooking and eating our meal we were all in bed by 7pm, and soon asleep.

We awoke at 5am to find ourselves in the clouds, very cold and damp. So after a quick breakfast we set off on a wet and slippery trail, passing two beaver ponds on the way to Story Spring shelter where we stopped for a break before the long climb up Stratton Mountain (3,936'). It is said that it was while sitting in a tree on the summit of Stratton Mountain that Benton MacKaye first envisaged a footpath running the length of the Appalachians, which he could see stretching away to north and south. You can now get a similar view by climbing the fire tower on the summit. After the long descent the trail reaches Stratton Pond, the most visited site on the AT in Vermont. The two shelters beside the pond are in a beautiful position, but we were very disappointed at the tatty condition of them. We settled in to Bigelow shelter and made lunch, but were plagued by mosquitoes. We tried to light a fire but the wood was too wet after the rain of the previous few days, so we went for a walk round the pond to take photographs and to get away from the bugs. The trail along the shore was very rough and poorly maintained so we were unable to get all the way round and returned the way we had come. We then persevered in our attempt to light a fire and finally got one going, which helped to disperse the mosquitoes. Ed arrived at about 7pm and we sat around the fire chatting while he cooked his meal, before retiring to bed shortly after 8 o'clock.

We awoke to a beautiful morning with a gentle mist rising from the surface of the pond. There was no rush to get away as we were only planning to hike ten miles to the road, where we hoped to hitch a lift to Manchester Center for a couple of nights in town. It was an easy section of trail, partly on an old dirt road and we arrived at the highway at 11.20am. After eating our lunch and tidying ourselves up in the parking area we went to the roadside to hitch a lift. It took about 25 minutes before somebody stopped - a lady in a Saab Turbo. We squeezed into the back seat of the car with our big packs, as there was a large dog in the front passenger seat, for the 5.5 mile ride to Manchester. There we were dropped right at the door of the Zion Episcopal Church which has a hikers' hostel. We were made very welcome by Rev. Jim Rains, his wife and secretary and were shown to the very spacious church hall where we could stay, with the use of a lounge, kitchen and bathrooms. After settling in we explored the town, which is a popular ski resort, and visited the usual attractions - laundry, post office and supermarket! We also discovered Mountain Goat, a very good outdoors shop with a large selection of hiking and backpacking supplies. After a superb steak dinner at the Sirloin Saloon we returned to the hostel and retired to bed at 9.30pm, feeling very overfed! We had the hostel to ourselves as Ed was spending the weekend with his girlfriend, Karen, and no other hikers had arrived.

We cooked bacon sandwiches for breakfast and spent a leisurely morning finishing our shopping and writing postcards. In the afternoon we met Ed and Karen in the laundromat and invited them back to the hostel for afternoon tea. Then we all went out together for dinner and spent a most enjoyable evening.

Next morning we took a taxi back to the trail in torrential rain, which continued for the rest of the day and night. We climbed Bromley Mountain (3,260') into the cloud and could only just make out the observation tower and summit buildings of the chair-lift. After passing over the second summit we took the side trail to Mad Tom shelter for a rest out of the rain and found several people camping there. It was an enclosed cabin and was very cosy. The occupants, who had spent the night there, made some hot-chocolate for us which warmed us up and, after about half an hour, we continued on our way.

In places the trail was several inches deep with water where the water-bars were blocked with fallen leaves. We managed to clear some, but didn't stop for too long in the awful weather. After Styles Peak (3,394') there was a steep drop into the col before beginning the climb to the summit of Peru Peak (3,429'), then a descent on switchbacks to Peru Peak shelter, where we arrived at 1pm after hiking 10 miles. The weather showed no sign of improving so we decided to stay there. It was great to change into dry clothes and after lunch we got into our sleeping-bags to keep warm. Ed arrived shortly afterwards, and did the same. We were well organised with all our wet gear hanging up to dry when a group of ten young hikers from Princeton University arrived for the night. After hiking all day they were absolutely soaked. We learned later that they were on an outdoor survival course and on that day they were learning about hypothermia - and almost had practical experience. We all managed to squeeze into the available space and spent a very cosy night, although it was a bit tricky finding space to cook breakfast in the morning!

It was a new month, (flaming June!) but it was still raining when we set out and all the streams and rivers were roaring torrents, and the ground underfoot was very wet and slippery. After crossing the summit of Baker Peak (2,850') on slippery rock slabs we stopped for a short break at Lost Pond shelter. When we crossed Big Branch on a swinging suspension bridge the river was the colour of coffee as it roared and tumbled over the rocks beneath us. We stopped to talk to another crowd of young hikers at Big Branch shelter and we hoped that we weren't all heading for the same shelter for the night! We arrived at Little Rock Pond shelter, on a hillside above the beautiful pond, at 12.30pm and changed into our dry clothes before having lunch. Ed arrived about an hour later and after the rain stopped we were able to get a fire going and dry some clothes over it. No one else came for the night, the other two groups of hikers stopped elsewhere.

The sun came out in the morning and the rain had stopped, but for the next few days the rivers were in spate and the trail was wet and boggy. After descending from White Rocks Mountain we came to Roaring Brook, which lived up to it's name, but we managed to cross on some rocks a short distance from the trail. We stopped for lunch at the Minerva Hinchey shelter, before beginning the steep descent to Clarendon Gorge. Here we crossed high above Mill River on a narrow suspension bridge which rocked gently up and down with every step as we eyed the spectacular torrent below us. The bridge was built as a memorial to a young hiker who was washed away while fording the river in 1969, a sobering thought.

After crossing through a field of cows in the valley we found ourselves scrambling up a steep, rocky gully, which came as a surprise as the guide book described a road walk. The trail had obviously been recently relocated away from the road and was very steep and rugged. On reaching the top we could look back down into the valley and see the suspension bridge far below us. After following the blazes for a while we began to worry that we had missed Clarendon shelter, or maybe it had been moved after the relocation, but we came across it just as we were discussing whether to retrace our steps. It was 3 o'clock on a lovely sunny afternoon and we spread out all our damp gear to air in the sun while we relaxed after hiking a rugged 13 miles. Ed arrived later and we spent another sociable evening with him.

We were up early and away at 6.15 next morning as we were planning to hike more than 15 miles to the road at Sherburne Pass. After a steep climb over Beacon Hill there was a pleasant walk through pastures and over another ridge before descending to the valley where we took a road walk to avoid fording Cold River which can be waist deep and treacherous after heavy rain. This added to our total mileage, but if we had reached the river and been unable to cross we would have had to retrace our route and wasted even more time.

We took a break at Governor Clement shelter before beginning the four mile climb up Little Killington and Killington Peak (4,235'). The Appalachian Trail is routed below the summit to avoid the buildings of the ski development, but passes Cooper Lodge where we stopped for lunch at midday. The lodge is a lovely old stone structure, but suffers from over-use as many people travel to the area on the chair-lift creating problems of litter and vandalism. The glass windows used to regularly get broken, so have been replaced by sheets of plastic which were torn and flapping in the wind. We were pleased that we hadn't planned to spend the night there and soon continued on our way, down a very badly eroded rocky trail to Pico Camp. This is a very nice enclosed cabin with a beautiful view from the window to Killington Peak, which still had snow (man-made!) lying on one of the ski runs. We had arranged to wait for Ed at the cabin and then decide whether to stay or continue down to the road, where he had left his truck in the parking area at the trailhead.

It was 2pm, and we didn't expect Ed for a couple of hours, so we made ourselves comfortable and even cooked a meal of beef noodles. When Ed arrived at 4.30pm we all made a speedy descent down a well worn trail and drove to one of the many motels in this area of extensive ski developments. Later we went to the town of Rutland to buy supplies and in the evening we enjoyed a very good meal at Churchill's Restaurant before returning to the motel and to bed at 10pm.

Next morning, after hiking little more than half a mile, we waved farewell to Ed at Maine Junction, the point where the Long Trail continues north to Canada and the AT heads north-east towards Maine. We had enjoyed his company and later heard that he completed his hike of the Long Trail sixteen days later at the Canadian border on 20th June.

For the next four days we were at lower elevations, crossing from the Green Mountains in Vermont to the White Mountain range in New Hampshire. After walking through Gifford Woods State Park and along the edge of Kent Pond we came to an area where the trail had been recently rerouted, but we had no trouble following the white blazes.

We hiked over a wooded ridge before descending to cross the

Ottauquechee River on a road bridge, then came a long climb on switchbacks up Quimby Mountain, followed by a sometimes tricky descent on the new trail to arrive at Stony Brook shelter at 1pm. We had only hiked 8.3 miles, but the weather was very hot and tiring so we decided to stay there. After lunch we had a refreshing wash, and also washed our smelly socks and "smalls" before relaxing in the sun. At 3pm Dan, a young hiker from northern Vermont, arrived. He had met Ed earlier in the day and had been expecting to catch up with us before too long.

The next day was cooler with a breeze as we hiked the nine miles along an undulating ridge through trees and on woods roads all the way to Wintturi shelter. We were there by 11.30am, but we had told Dan that we would meet him there so we lit a fire and made ourselves at home. It turned quite cool so we prepared a hot lunch, a real luxury. Dan arrived at 1.30pm, followed by two more hikers at 4 o'clock so we rearranged our gear to make room for them. They were Dave and Bill from Boston, out for a few days hiking. Rain was forecast, but we got a good big fire burning and spent a very pleasant evening with good company.

It rained all night and was continuing when we awoke at 5.45am, so we didn't rush too much. Our three companions stayed in their sleeping bags while we made breakfast and packed our rucksacks. They were just beginning to get up when we left at 8 o'clock, by which time the rain had almost stopped. It was very pleasant hiking through the damp woods and over gentle hills, some of which were clear of trees so we had views of the misty hills all around, and honeysuckle was growing in many of the clearings smelling very sweet in the dampness.

We walked a mile down the road to the small village of South Pomfret to visit the general store and post office, passing a ski area with the intriguing name of Suicide Six en route. It was Saturday morning and we met several local people in the store who all seemed happy to pass the time of day with us while we ate hot-dogs and salad and drank many cups of coffee. When we were ready to leave a lady gave us a lift back to the trail, which continued through a beautiful pine forest with very tall straight trees and a soft carpet of pine needles underfoot.

After descending to cross a road we followed the blazes up the side of a pasture and found the side trail to Cloudland shelter, which we reached at 2pm. Shortly afterwards twelve members of the Green Mountain Club, which maintains the Appalachian and Long Trails in Vermont, arrived on a day hike so we had a long discussion with them. They went on their way just after Dan arrived, so we went about our usual chores and managed to get a good fire going despite the wet wood.

We were all up at 5am next morning for the 17 mile walk to Norwich, where Dan would complete his few days on the Trail. It was very humid and there were lots of mosquitoes about so we made good use of our insect repellent. They didn't seem to bother us when we were on the move, but rapidly found us when we stopped, so we kept going!

The trail undulated over gentle hills before descending to cross the bridge over the White River at West Hartford, where we stopped for a snack at the Country Store. Then we continued on the trail, over the railroad and under the interstate highway, before climbing steeply up through the woods to pass over Griggs Mountain and arrive at Happy Hill Cabin, the oldest shelter on the Appalachian Trail (built in 1917). This could have been a beautiful place to stay, but the lovely big cabin had been badly vandalised and there were piles of empty beer cans all around (apparently it is often used for beer parties by local youths as it is very close to a road). So after a short rest we continued down the trail to Norwich and booked in to the Norwich Inn.

New Hampshire : 9 June - 25 June.

We crossed the Connecticut River to the university town of Hanover, New Hampshire on 9th June and spent a night at the Occum Inn. John had arranged for Chuck to send a new pair of boots for collection at the post office, so we collected the parcel and found that there were two pairs in it! We packaged up the spare pair and forwarded them to Gorham (just in case they would be needed further along the Trail), then did our shopping and found some very nice restaurants and bars (including one which sold Murphy's Stout on draught, a real treat for John!).

Also in Hanover we visited the office of the Dartmouth Outing Club which maintains the Appalachian Trail in this area. We enquired about staying at the "Atwell Hilton", a house owned by the club and used as a summer base by their trail-maintaining crews. Thru'-hikers are allowed to stay there as there is no shelter in that area, but as it had not yet been opened up for the summer season we were told that we could put up our tent on the lawn when we arrived in the area in a couple of day's time.

It has been said that when a northbound thru'-hiker reaches New Hampshire he has completed 80% of the Appalachian Trail, but still has 50% of the work to do. We would agree, the hard work starts here! From Hanover the Trail heads in a north-easterly direction, climbing towards the White Mountains where, for the next 100 strenuous miles, it climbs over high, rugged peaks with deep notches between.

We were up early to return to the trail and were waiting outside Lou's Diner when it opened at 6am! It was a bright, cool morning and after a good breakfast we were on our way following the blazes through the middle of Hanover, past the high school and supermarket to the gas station, where we turned along the edge of the sports field before leaving civilization to climb the ridge.

When we reached a large beaver pond we were surprised to find that the AT went straight across the dam, with no way to avoid it. This was rather disconcerting, so we very cautiously took a few steps on to the long pile of sticks which was holding back the large volume of water. But we need not have worried, it was surprisingly strong and sturdy and we applauded the engineering ability of these animals. We stopped several times along the trail as John's feet were giving him trouble, and whenever we stopped we were attacked by swarms of mosquitoes. So it was not a very pleasant morning. We met "Greyman's Lantern", the first southbound thru'-hiker to have come all the way from Mount Katahdin, and chatted with him for a while exchanging information about the sections of the Trail we had hiked.

After climbing to the South Peak of Moose Mountain (2,290') we descended to the col and then took the side trail to Moose Mountain shelter, where we arrived at 12.15 after hiking 12 miles. It is a strange shelter with a very low roof overhang which we had to duck under to get in and out. John was very worried about his feet as he thought he may be having a recurrence of the problem which had forced us off the Trail in 1990, so we were not very happy hikers that day.

We were awake early and back on the trail before 7am to continue over the North Peak of Moose Mountain, then a steep 1,400' descent before crossing another beaver dam - no problem! After climbing back up 1,000' to Holts Ledge we managed to lose our way and found ourselves at the top of a ski tow, so we had to retrace our steps along the ledge before finding the way down beside a ski trail. After reaching the road we began the long 2,360' climb up Smarts Mountain (3,240') along rough, rocky ledges with a very steep section to reach the summit. We reached the disused firewarden's cabin at 2.10pm after hiking 13.7 miles and climbing 3,900'. We were relieved that John's foot had not been too painful and had coped well with the climbs.

We spent the night in the cabin, which was quite cosy, and next day had a long descent into the valley before climbing Mount Cube (2,911') over rocky ledges with good views. It was very warm and sunny with a nice breeze, but when we descended again it was very hot and as we passed through a large swampy area we received the attentions of clouds of mosquitoes. After this we arrived at the "Atwell Hilton" and found that the "lawn" we had permission to camp on consisted of grass and weeds some 18" high! But as it was so hot, and the mosquitoes were bothering us, we found a flat area and put up the tent. Fortunately the outside water tap was working, but we spent a most uncomfortable time there - if we stayed outside we were eaten alive by the mozzies and if we went in the tent it was stifling hot. Next morning we were up and away from this unpleasant place by 6am!

We had an easy hike of ten miles passing over Mount Mist (2,220') before following the road into the village of Glencliff. We visited the post office to mail a film and asked the postmaster if there was anywhere we could buy a drink. He phoned a neighbour who sometimes sells sodas and hot dogs from his front porch, and he agreed to set up shop for us. So, having spent a few more minutes chatting with the postmaster and his wife, we wandered up the road and there was Henry with his hot dog stand at the ready. Such personal service! We sat on the grass verge drinking cans of Coke, eating hot dogs and hearing the local gossip. It was a pleasant rest as the weather was hot and humid - very energy sapping.

When we returned to the trail we had a short walk to Jeffers Brook shelter where, although it was hot, we lit a fire to keep the mosquitoes away. We heard voices as several groups of people passed by, presumably on the forest road, and we thought some may have been planning a party at the shelter (it being a Saturday), but none came to disturb us and we had a peaceful night.

We were up at 5am and on the trail an hour later for the assault on Mount Moosilauke (4,802'), the first of the White Mountains. This involved a five mile climb of 3,500' which we completed in 3 hours and 5 minutes, including a stop of 20 minutes near the summit of South Peak so that John could wring out his sweat-soaked T-shirt! The views ahead to the rest of the Whites were hazy, and the 3,000' descent was very steep. In places wooden steps and iron hand rails had been bolted to the sheer rocks, but it was very pretty descending beside long cascades and waterfalls.

When we reached the road at Kinsman Notch (gaps are called notches in New England) we walked along the road to a cafe for refreshment. From here we phoned Betty Robinson, the owner of Cascade Lodge in North Woodstock, where we were to spend two nights. She came out to pick us up and drive us the six miles to town. Next day we were returned to the trail carrying only enough gear for one night out (leaving the rest at the hotel) so that we could "slack-pack" to the next notch.

Although the trail was rugged, with a steep 1,000' climb out of Kinsman Notch, we arrived at Eliza Brook shelter at noon and got a good campfire going as a cold north wind was blowing. Next morning we climbed away from the shelter on a rough, steep trail beside the beautiful cascades of Eliza Brook then continued the 2,000' climb with some scrambles to the twin peaks of Mount Kinsman (4,358' and 4,293'). From the open, rocky summits there were wonderful views down to Kinsman Pond and ahead over the Whites.

It was a long, steep descent to Lonesome Lake Hut, one of the series of mountain lodges in the White Mountains operated by the Appalachian Mountain Club. They provide meals and basic lodging in very remote locations and are run by "croos" of very competent college age youngsters. We called in and chatted with the "croo" then continued on our way, passing beautiful Lonesome Lake, down to Franconia Notch where we got a lift back to our hotel at North Woodstock.

Betty took us back to the trail early next morning, as we had a long, rugged day ahead of us, and we were on our way at 6am. Out of Franconia Notch there is a climb of 3,000' in 2.5 miles, but we managed this in two hours despite carrying our full packs again.

It was a beautiful sunny day with wonderful visibility so the views from Franconia Ridge were tremendous. This ridge is above treeline for two miles and scrambles over Little Haystack Mountain (4,760'), Mount Lincoln (5,089') and Mount Lafayette (5,249'). After spending most of the preceding 1,800 miles of the AT in woods it was wonderful to have reached this open, airy ridge on such a glorious day. We met several hikers up here, most of them had been staying at the nearby Greenleaf Hut, located on a spur about a mile off the Trail.

From the summit of Mount Lafayette it was a long, rocky way down to Garfield Pond, where we ate our lunch, before climbing up again over Mount Garfield (4,488') and then down to Galehead Hut, where we had booked accommodation. We had hiked 13.6 long, rocky miles and were very tired, but it was well worth the effort. It was a very satisfying day, rounded off by an excellent meal and good company at the hut. After dinner there was a talk given by Mac Nason, an AMC naturalist, which was very interesting and informative.

After a large breakfast we waited for the hut "croo" to make their morning radio call when they were able to see if there was accommodation available for us at the next hut. There was, so we set off for a leisurely hike as it was only 7 miles to Zealand Falls Hut. After an initial climb of 1,000' we were again on rocky ridges and summits with extensive views of the mountains all around us.

We stopped for lunch at a beautiful viewpoint and arrived at Zealand Falls at 1.30pm. The hut is situated in a most dramatic setting next to the cascades of a beautiful stream, where you can sit or lie on the rock slabs with the water tumbling all around you, and marvel at the

Franconia Ridge, NH
White Mountains, NH

wonderful view down to Zealand Pond sparkling way below. We had met several hikers who were doing day-hikes from hut-to-hut and one young couple who were hiking through the White Mountains to Lonesome Lake Hut where they were to be married in two day's time. Many people arrived throughout the afternoon while we were relaxing in the warm sunshine on the rocks in the river.

Next day was an easy hike along the bed of an old logging-railroad before dropping down into Crawford Notch where we walked along the road to the AMC hostel to spend the night. It was a warm, humid day but was to be our last day of good weather for a week, so we saw none of the spectacular views from the Presidential Range as it was shrouded in cloud and rain.

The 25 mile section from Crawford Notch to Pinkham Notch is generally above 4,000', with many peaks over 5,000' and Mount Washington at 6,288'. It is mostly above treeline with the trail marked by cairns, and is subject to sudden and violent changes in weather. There is a notice on Mount Washington telling of the highest wind ever observed by man being recorded there on 12th April, 1934. The wind speed recorded was 231 miles per hour - and then the anemometer blew away! We felt fortunate to have hiked this section in good weather on a previous occasion, so we did not wait for the weather to clear, but plodded on. We passed Lake of the Clouds Hut where we had planned to stay and got a ride down the motor road from the top of Mount Washington. (Both the narrow, winding road and a cog-railway take tourists to the summit of the highest mountain in the north-eastern United States.)

The weather was no better the next day when we returned to continue our traverse. The trail follows the high and rugged horseshoe of the northern Presidential Range with a very steep descent of over 3,000' in 2.4 miles from the summit of Mount Madison (5,363'). When we arrived at Pinkham Notch Camp the accommodation was full with hikers waiting for an improvement in the weather, so we got a lift into the town of Gorham and took bed and breakfast at Gorham House.

The weather was forecast to improve next day so, after an excellent breakfast cooked by the owner, Ron Orso, we got a ride back to the trail and had a wet and slippery climb to Carter Notch Hut. This is situated in high and remote Carter Notch, a rugged pass in the mountains, between Wildcat Mountain (4,422') and Carter Dome (4,832'). It had stopped raining by the time we arrived so, after a short rest, we were able to enjoy the solitude of this rugged area, scrambling among huge boulders with ice still lying in the hollows, and relaxing beside the two beautiful little lakes. It was a great place to spend the night with eight other hikers and a super "croo".

We planned to spend the next night at Imp shelter, but we arrived there by lunchtime after a strenuous 7 miles with a steep climb to Carter Dome, followed by a rugged hike over the Carter Range. It was again wet and cloudy so we decided to continue down to Gorham, rather than sit in the cold, damp clouds all afternoon. On the summit of Mount Moriah (4,049') we had difficulty locating the trail, but we eventually found our way and descended to Gorham on the very steep and slippery Carter-Moriah Trail, which led us directly into the town, over a rickety suspension bridge, near Gorham House. Ron was surprised to see us again so soon as we were not due back until the next day, but he made us very welcome and we decided to stay two nights and do all our chores.

There were three hikers, "The Swille Dogs", staying in the barn, which Ron has opened for hikers to camp in, and later two southbounders arrived. Their names were Liz and Philip, so we gave them the trailname "The Young Royals". Ron offered us the use of his truck, so we went to the nearby town of Berlin for dinner and, next day drove round Gorham doing our laundry and shopping. We collected the parcel of boots which we had forwarded from Hanover and John wore them for the rest of the Trail, with no further discomfort.

Next day, after a wonderful breakfast of fresh fruit and blueberry pancakes, Ron drove us back to the trailhead. As we climbed up from the valley on a wet and boggy trail the cloud was clearing and we had good views back to the Presidential Range. Before reaching Gentian Pond shelter there was a long wet section with broken bog bridges, making for very uncomfortable hiking. We found The Swille Dogs at the shelter, but they decided to continue further so we were on our own for the night. There was a beautiful view from the shelter when we arrived, but the cloud soon rolled in so we lit a fire and cooked a meal before snuggling into our sleeping bags for our last night in New Hampshire.

Maine : 25 June - 21 July.

On 25th June we passed the sign board marking the state line and crossed into Maine, the final state on the Appalachian Trail. Only 275 miles to go, but we had been told that the next 110 miles are the toughest yet, starting with the infamous Mahoosuc Notch and then considerable gain and loss of height as the trail traverses seven peaks over 4,000' and nine more over 3,000'. After this rugged section there would be easy hiking for 53 miles before entering the "100 mile wilderness" on the approach to our goal - Baxter Peak, the summit of Mount Katahdin and the northern terminus of the Appalachian Trail.

It was still damp and cloudy as we began our traverse of the Mahoosuc Range, with peaks between 3,500' and 4,000'. It began with the very tricky descent down steep and slippery rocks into Carlo Col and an equally steep climb out again and up Mount Carlo (3,562'). After descending there followed the three peaks of Goose Eye Mountain, with steep descents and climbs; we had to slide down one area on our backsides as the rock was too steep to keep a footing.

After hiking 9.6 miles we arrived at Full Goose lean-to (shelters are called lean-tos in Maine) where we again met The Swille Dogs, and shortly afterwards were joined by a young couple (Peter and Julie) whom we had passed on Goose Eye Mountain. We all decided to stay the night there and we were later joined by a group of twelve schoolboys, two teachers and an outdoor pursuits instructor from Newry in Northern Ireland. The boys put up their tents and the rest of us slept in the shelter; it was a most unusual ratio of 17 Brits to 5 Americans that night!

Next morning was dry and cool, and we were up early to get away before the crowd. We were soon joined on the trail by Peter and Julie and we would hike together through another notch, but one that is like no other - Mahoosuc Notch. We had read and heard stories about this place, and now we were there to see for ourselves. Unlike most of the other notches on the Appalachian Trail, Mahoosuc Notch has no road passing through it, in fact there is not even a footpath, just the white blazes suggesting a way over, under and round the jumble of huge boulders which have fallen from the steep high cliffs on either side.

The notch is only a mile long and a few metres wide, but it took the four of us two hours to thread our way through this maze as we squeezed ourselves and our big packs through narrow cracks, hauled ourselves up sheer rocks and stretched across chasms with frozen snow still visible way down in the bottom. This isn't a place to hurry, a fall or injury here would be disastrous. But we made steady progress, taking time to assess each move and it's consequences as in a game of chess, making it an exhilarating and satisfying challenge. It was worth stopping a while to look up at the narrow patch of sky above, to feel like an ant in a trough of gravel, and to wonder at the tough stunted trees and shrubs growing in this inhospitable place, their roots and branches making welcome hand holds and foot steps to help us through the obstacle course.

It had been cool and damp in the notch, but the sun was out when we emerged and we had a short rest before tackling the long, steep climb up Mahoosuc Arm. We arrived at Speck Pond lean-to after hiking only five miles in 6 hours. We didn't feel like continuing another five miles to the next shelter so we stayed there and were again joined by all our companions of the previous night. There was a heavy shower in the afternoon so late-comers arrived very wet, but everyone was in high spirits after their adventures in The Notch and we spent the evening recalling our experiences. We were pestered by black flies, but the boys built a good campfire, so we sat in the smoke - that being preferable to being eaten alive! It was a most entertaining evening.

Next day began with a steep climb up Old Speck Mountain (4,180') followed by a three mile descent of 2,400' to Grafton Notch. After crossing the road we took a side trail to Grafton Notch lean-to, where we met four campers who had parked their car at the road and carried vast supplies to the shelter. They made us cups of coffee before we continued on our way over the two peaks of Baldpate Mountain (3,680' & 3,812'). This was a most enjoyable day of climbs over rocky summits with good views, and masses of alpine flowers blooming in lovely warm, sunny weather.

After a night at Frye Notch lean-to we had a short hike to Dunn Notch Falls, where we met a group of French-Canadian students who gave us a lift in their mini-bus to the small town of Andover. There we arrived at Pine Ellis b & b at 9.20am on a Sunday morning and were made very welcome by the owners Paul and Ilene Trainor. After sitting round the kitchen table with them drinking coffee they asked if we would mind being left on our own as they had planned to visit relations in Vermont. We did not mind at all, but were surprised that they would leave complete strangers alone in their house - with instructions to help ourselves to any food and drink, and to show anyone else who arrived to the rooms. So, we were left in charge and spent a lovely day, doing our laundry and relaxing in the garden. Marc and Paul (two of The

Swille Dogs - one had gone off the Trail), arrived for the night, and in the evening Paul and Ilene cooked us a super steak dinner.

Paul gave us a lift back to the trail next morning and we hiked with light packs to the next road crossing where he picked us up again in the afternoon. We saw our first moose that day as we were making the gentle ascent of Wyman Mountain (2,945'). It ambled up the trail ahead of us and kept turning round to look at us, but it soon became bored and wandered off into the woods, where it stood to watch us pass. We stopped for lunch at Hall Mountain lean-to before the steep descent into Sawyer Notch, followed by an equally steep climb on rocky ledges up Moody Mountain. From the cliffs at the top we stopped to look back at Hall Mountain, with the sheer drop of 1,100' into Sawyer Notch between. We descended to Black Brook, which we crossed on rocks, and then sat beside the road until Paul arrived to take us back to Andover. We showered and did some shopping in the general store before going out for a meal with Marc and Paul, who had taken a day off the Trail.

We saw two more moose (a mother and calf) the next morning when Paul was driving us back to the trail, they crossed the road in front of us with no roadsense whatever. We could well see why these animals are the cause of so many road traffic accidents in New Hampshire and Maine. We were again "slack-packing" and made good time up the steep climb to the summit of Old Blue Mountain (3,600') before beginning the traverse of the Bemis Range (with five summits between 2,500' and 3,500'). The weather was fine in the morning, but it started to rain heavily just as we arrived at Bemis Mountain lean-to for lunch. By the time we were ready to set off again it had almost stopped and stayed dry for the rest of the day - excellent timing!

We passed several hikers making their way up the Bemis Range from the north as we made our way down to the valley, where we crossed the route of an old railroad before crossing both branches of

Bemis Brook on rocks. It was then a short, steep climb up to the road where Paul was again to meet us. Two other hikers had arrived at Pine Ellis when we returned and Ilene had cooked us another lovely meal.

We saw many hikers on the trail in Maine, and passed the first southbound thru'-hikers (who don't start from Katahdin until late May due to the late winter weather this far north). We also encountered more wildlife, which seemed to be of a different temperament than further south. The animals and birds did not appear to be afraid of us and we were able to quietly watch them from close quarters, as they watched us. The moose was the largest and most impressive of these northern animals; they never ran off or threatened us but, after watching us for a while, they would lose interest and wander off into the woods.

We also encountered spruce grouse on several occasions which, instead of exploding from the undergrowth and zooming off at high speed as the ruffed grouse did in the south, these more colourful northern cousins would stand their ground on the trail in front of us. After looking us up and down they would walk on up the trail keeping just a few feet ahead, looking back from time to time to see if we were still there. The chipping sparrow had a similar habit, but instead of staying on the trail it would land on a low branch, wait for us to come almost level with it then fly a few more yards to another branch. This could continue for a hundred yards or more as if it was guiding us through it's territory.

Another interesting bird was the Canada (gray) jay, which often flew down to see if we were a likely source of food and has earned the name "camp robber" as it is so bold and will even take food from a hand. Even the chipmunks and squirrels, which we had seen all along the Appalachian Trail, were more bold in Maine, actually coming into shelters and investigating rucksacks and food bags right under our noses. Even when they were threatened with a stick they would just hide briefly then reappear just as boldly.

We also saw many toads and frogs in our path and we had to be careful where we placed our feet for, again, they just did not move out of the way.

One bird which we heard on many occasions in Maine was the loon (great northern diver), but we never saw one. When we were staying near a pond or lake we would be lying in our sleeping bags at dusk when they would start calling across the water, sometimes an eerie yodelling and at other times a raucous laugh! All these animals added to our enjoyment of Maine, we felt privileged to be accepted by them as a fellow creature in the woods.

We left Andover on 1st July and hiked for 13 miles over a ridge, skirting several lovely ponds. We stopped for a break at Sabbath Pond lean-to and for lunch in a clearing beside Little Swift River Pond, where we chatted with two fishermen while we filled our water bottles from a spring near the shore. We made good time down to the road in the valley as we were running short of cash and hoped to get to Rangeley before the bank closed. We were at the road by 2pm, and very soon got a lift into town where we checked into a motel and got to the bank in good time. Then we could relax for the rest of the afternoon, before treating ourselves to an excellent dinner at the Rangeley Inn.

The motel manager gave us an early lift back to the trail in the morning so we were on our way again before 7am for the climb up Saddleback (4,116'), again passing ponds and bogs. It was a beautiful sunny day and when we came out above treeline the view down to Rangeley, and beyond to the mountains we had hiked over on the previous few days, was quite stunning. The trail was above treeline for three miles and we hiked over smooth granite with masses of alpine flowers and stunted shrubs in full bloom. From the summit of Saddleback the view was wonderful, as well as seeing back the way we had come, we could now look ahead to Sugarloaf, our next destination.

Saddleback summit, ME
Bogs!

We passed over the summits of the Horn (4,023') and Saddleback Junior (3,640') before descending through the trees to Poplar Ridge lean-to. This is one of the few remaining "baseball-bat" shelters (i.e. with floors made of pine saplings, creating a sleeping surface rather like the top of a roll-top desk!). The floors of these shelters are gradually being replaced with conventional planks, but we did not find it too uncomfortable through our Thermorest mattresses. Five other hikers joined us for the night, but they all decided to sleep in their tents as the shelter looked too uncomfortable!

We awoke early as usual after a good nights sleep, and while packing we chatted with Peter and Sandy, two of the other hikers, about the possibility of spending the night in the summit house on Sugarloaf Mountain.

It was another warm, sunny day as we set off down the steep descent into a deep valley to cross Orbeton Stream, which we forded on rocks with support from long poles we found on the bank. After a long climb over Lone Mountain (3,280') we stopped for lunch at Spaulding Mountain lean-to, then continued up Spaulding Mountain (3,988'), seeing two moose ahead of us shortly before the summit. As we had come to expect, they sauntered up the trail ahead of us, then wandered off into the woods, stopping to look back and watch us pass.

The AT bypasses Sugarloaf Mountain (4,237'), but we had arranged to meet Peter and Sandy there so we took the steep, rocky side-trail to the summit, stopping to collect water at a spring on the way. We crossed the boulder-field to the summit-house, which we found to be open, so we went inside and up to the top-floor were we decided to stay for the night. Peter and Sandy had told us that hikers were welcome to use the building, which is the terminus of the ski-gondola, and recommended it as it has one of the best views in Maine. The visibility was perfect and from the panoramic windows we could see our ultimate goal, Mount Katahdin 100 miles to the north, and we could also see the

White Mountains back in New Hampshire, one-sixth of the Appalachian Trail! It was well worth the detour to see the wonderful views on this perfect day.

Peter and Sandy arrived later as they had detoured to take in another summit. We cooked our meal and laid out our sleeping-bags on the floor, and were then joined by three southbound hikers. During the night we were awoken by the howling wind and torrential rain lashing at the windows, and when daylight arrived it was still raining and we were in the clouds. We waited until about 9 o'clock, when the wind and rain had decreased somewhat and then the four of us set off to slip and slide down the mountain on one of the ski-trails, which meant that we would avoid fording the Carrabassett River. The southbound hikers had told us that the water was high the previous day and after the torrential overnight rain would be almost impossible to ford.

The wind had decreased, but the rain continued as we made our way to the small town of Stratton, where we spent the night at the Stratton Motel. The cloud was still low next morning as we climbed up the Bigelow Range, but when we emerged above the clouds we could see the top of Sugarloaf across the valley. The open summit of West Peak (4,150') was rough and rocky, with good views down over Flagstaff Lake to the north of the ridge as the cloud continued to lift. In the col between the two main peaks of the Bigelows is the Myron Avery lean-to, named in memory of one of the founders of the AT. We decided to stay there as the cloud was coming down again and it got very cold, so we lit a fire, had an early meal and snuggled in our sleeping-bags by 6pm.

The cloud had dispersed by morning so we climbed up to the firetower on Avery Peak (4,088'), with excellent views all around as we crossed the rocky summit amongst the tiny alpine plants. Then a long descent into Safford Notch passing huge boulders before climbing up and along the undulating crest of Little Bigelow Mountain in the sunshine. We passed several southbound hikers making their way up the ridge, as we descended to pass the end of Flagstaff Lake. We were climbing Roundtop Mountain when it started raining, but it had stopped by the time we reached West Carry Pond, where we settled into the new lean-to above the shore after hiking 13.9 miles.

Next day was easy hiking with no mountains to climb, but the trail was rough with plenty of rocks and roots as we skirted West and East Carry Ponds and crossed several boggy areas on bog bridges. After hiking only 9.7 miles we arrived early at Pierce Pond where there is a hunting and fishing camp run by Fran and Tim Harrison. This has become a legend with AT hikers because of the huge breakfasts available there so, after unloading our gear in Pierce Pond lean-to, we followed the blue-blazed trail the half-mile to Harrison Camp to book our breakfast for the following morning.

The main building is a beautiful wooden lodge overlooking the spectacular cascades of Pierce Pond Stream, and accommodation is available to visitors in rustic cabins. We booked our meal and returned to the shelter via the AT, crossing over the very precarious dam at the outlet to the pond. In the evening we sat beside the pond and watched the fishermen going out for an evening's sport, and saw a moose browsing in the shallows. As it got dark we heard the eerie calls of the loons. This was an idyllic setting, just how we had imagined Maine.

Next morning we could have a lie-in, as breakfast was booked for 7.30, so we had a leisurely cup of tea in bed before packing our gear and leaving this lovely shelter. We had a pleasant walk over to Harrison Camp, taking a short detour to view the waterfall, but still arrived early so we spent some time chatting with guests who were staying at the camp, and also watching tiny humming birds feeding outside the window. Breakfast was served in the dining room of the lodge, overlooking Pierce Pond Stream and decorated with many hunting trophies, including "Bruce the Moose"! The breakfast came up to expectations - John ordered pancakes with sausage and eggs, Pam had pancakes and sausage. After our orange juice, the big oval platters arrived, each loaded with thirteen (a baker's dozen) pancakes. They were delicious and John managed to eat all of his, but Pam had to admit defeat after ten. All this was washed down with plenty of excellent coffee, just what we needed to set us up for the day ahead. After this feast it was rather uncomfortable buckling our hipbelts, but we had to be on our way as the next highlight of the Appalachian Trail was only three miles away - the Kennebec River.

The trail followed the beautiful Pierce Pond Stream, passing several waterfalls, as it tumbled down to the Kennebec, the crossing of which is legend in AT circles. There is no bridge and until 1986 hikers had to ford this wide river, which could be chest deep and very unpredictable as a dam upstream releases water automatically when power is needed. After a hiker was drowned in 1985 the ATC and Maine ATC arranged for a local rafting company to provide a ferry service between 10am and noon each day during the main hiking season. Some thru'-hikers still prefer the challenge of fording the river, but we arrived at the crossing just before 10 o'clock and raised the orange signal to alert the ferryman when he arrived on the far bank. We sat down to enjoy the sunshine, but within 5 minutes we saw the canoe setting out from the opposite side. The canoe only carries one passenger and a rucksack at a time, so Pam went first and then the friendly ferryman returned for John. It was a really pleasant voyage on a beautiful sunny day, but even in these perfect conditions we would not have been keen to ford the river.

We were greeted on the far bank by a group of youngsters heading south - they were the French-Canadians who had given us a ride into Andover ten days previously! We were planning to walk up the road to the small village of Caratunk to buy supplies in the general store, so the group's leader joined us and we bought tubs of ice-cream for them all to thank them for the lift in their vehicle.

After restocking with groceries we walked out of Caratunk in the warm sunshine, sharing a large tub of ice-cream. The next shelter was only six miles up the trail, so we had a leisurely hike although the trail was quite rough in places as it had recently been relocated and hadn't yet worn in. The relocation has taken the trail off a road and it now follows Holly Brook, crossing it on several occasions.

The sky started to cloud over and it began raining just before we reached Pleasant Pond lean-to, which was occupied by a family out on a day hike. We chatted with them while they ate their lunch and the two young boys were very excited about what we were doing, later announcing that they would hike the whole AT when they were old enough! After they left we unpacked our gear and did the usual chores. We had read that "The Cookie Lady" often leaves goodies at this shelter when she is out walking and, sure enough, in a large tin were some home-made pecan cookies as well as another tin with packs of snack biscuits, rice, pasta and parmesan cheese. What a wonderful person to do this for strangers she will never meet. The cookies went down very well with our afternoon tea - a British tradition we maintained all along the Trail, to the amusement of some of the American hikers.

That evening a young southbound hiker (Bob) arrived with his dog, which was very well-behaved and slept under the shelter. We spent a pleasant evening discussing trail conditions ahead (in both directions), and then early to bed as we were planning an early start next day. At about 2am we were awakened by torrential rain beating on the shelter roof, and this continued for the rest of the night. When we awoke at 5am we made a cup of tea, but stayed in our sleeping-bags and listened to the weather forecast on a small radio which we were carrying for that purpose. As they were predicting that the rain would continue until early afternoon we decided to stay at the shelter for the day and another night, rather than rushing over two mountains on a wet and slippery trail. Bob also decided to stay as he had to cross the Kennebec and thought the ferry may not be operating in the bad conditions.

We spent a very pleasant day with good company, just talking, reading, eating, drinking and dozing in our sleeping-bags. We later realised that this was the only real day of rest we had on the whole Trail (our days off in towns were spent doing shopping, laundry, etc). The rain did eventually stop around midday so in the afternoon we went out to stretch our legs and gather some firewood. We managed to find some that was not too wet and eventually got a good fire going. Bob then produced three potatoes out of his rucksack and we baked them in the fire and ate them with our beef noodles, a delicious meal. Then another short walk down to the pond before bed. It had turned out to be a very pleasant day and we felt revitalised after the enforced rest.

Next day we were pleased that we had waited to hike this section in good weather as there were magnificent views. The climb up Pleasant Pond Mountain was steep in places, but not as bad as some of the entries in the register had led us to believe, and we managed to cross the fast flowing Baker Brook on rocks rather than on the cable bridge which looked very precarious (one cable for the feet and one for the hands). We stopped for lunch at Joe's Hole lean-to, but were soon on our way again as it was a miserable place, very dark and damp with lots of mosquitoes. We were very pleased that we hadn't planned to spend the night there. Then another steep climb up Moxie Bald Mountain in good weather with superb views from the top before descending to Moxie Bald Mountain Pond where we spent the night at the shelter near the shore, having hiked 12.3 strenuous miles.

We had been in our sleeping-bags about ten minutes when we saw a shadowy figure moving through the trees between us and the pond. It was a moose. She wandered past the shelter, then we heard splashing in the water so we got up and went to the shore and watched as she browsed on the weed in the shallows. After taking photographs we went back to bed and were entertained by a chipmunk gathering crumbs outside the shelter. We later watched the moose as it walked back along the edge of the pond. Quite an evening's entertainment!

The next day was again warm and sunny as we followed the trail along the edge of the pond before heading off into the woods, where it was quite overgrown in places. When we emerged from the trees on to a dirt road we met a couple camping there on a fishing expedition. They invited us to join them for coffee and we chatted with them for a while. They told us that the Piscataquis River was high and suggested that we should follow the logging road for the next few miles to avoid having to ford the river in two places. We took their advice and had a long, hot walk on the gravel road. We arrived in the town of Monson in time to visit the post office before it closed and collected some mail which we had asked to be sent there.

We went to Shaw's Boarding Home, an establishment famous among AT hikers. Keith and Pat Shaw have opened their home for hikers to stay, either in the bunkroom, private rooms or camping on the lawn. We took a room and were made very welcome. We met many hikers there, including Steve "Tenderfoot" Skokowski who was aiming to thru'-hike from Maine to Georgia, but had already spent three days in hospital and a week recuperating from trench foot, contracted during a very wet period prior to arriving in Monson. However, when we met him, he was ready to continue his hike and we wished him good luck.

A group of eleven young hikers from a summer camp arrived and set up their tents on the front lawn and, shortly afterwards, "Slo Jo" arrived (we had met her and her partner at Pine Ellis in Andover two weeks earlier). On the evening before we left Monson the first northbound thru'-hiker of the year arrived, his name was Lawrence "Fairhope". They were all very good company and we really enjoyed our two days at Shaw's while we prepared for the next section of the Trail - the "100-mile wilderness".

For nearly 100 miles north of Monson there is no habitation as the Appalachian Trail passes through very remote mountains and forests, with just two logging roads to provide a way out in emergency. Hikers are advised to carry enough food for ten days, consequently when we left Monson our packs weighed about 50lbs - the heaviest they had been. We had a late start as it was raining hard when we got up, but it was clearing by 10am so we went on our way.

At first it was easy going past several ponds, but the trail was very slippery as the exposed rock in this section is slate. After stopping to admire Little Wilson Falls in a deep canyon we crossed Little Wilson Stream on rocks then climbed up a ridge of slate and stopped for lunch on a sunny ledge with a beautiful view. After descending the ridge we should have forded Big Wilson Stream, but the water was very high and fast-flowing after the rain so, after studying it for some time, we decided to take a 6-mile detour on a dirt road to cross it on a bridge. We climbed up the ridge on the other side then had to cross Long Pond Stream to reach the shelter for the night. This stream also looked dangerous, but there was no way round so we each found two sturdy poles and looked for the best place to cross. We found a place downstream where it was wider and had an island in the middle so we set off from there, heading from one rock to the next and resting behind them out of the strong current. We made it to the other side and emptied the water out of our boots, but didn't bother to change our clothes (the water had been up to our shorts) as it was only one mile to Long Pond Stream lean-to. We arrived there at 7pm having hiked 16 miles and found that three southbound hikers were already installed. They made room for us and we just had time to cook our meal and make our beds before dark. Fairhope arrived at about 8.30, so it was a full shelter that night.

The next day we climbed up Barren Mountain (2,670'), the first of the five peaks of the rocky Barren-Chairback Range, which the Trail follows to Chairback Gap lean-to. It was a dull, cloudy day and the undulating trail was rough with many rocks and roots. Showers started around midday and it was raining steadily by the time we reached the shelter at 2.40 pm, having hiked only 9.7 miles and scrambled over

Fourth, Third and Columbus Mountains. There were very bold red squirrels at this shelter which were a real nuisance, coming in and investigating our rucksacks in broad daylight with us sitting there! We always hung up our food bags at night to keep them out of reach of the mice and fortunately this ploy worked for squirrels too and our precious food remained safe.

The weather was dry and bright when we set out the next morning, but the trees, trail and undergrowth were very wet. After a steep descent into Chairback Gap we climbed Chairback Mountain (2,197'), with good views from the rocky ledges at the top. Then down the "chairback cliffs" which gave the mountain it's name - a very steep scramble down large boulders. After climbing up and over three ridges we descended through thick forest to the West Branch of the Pleasant River. It was about 40 yards wide and knee deep, but we forded it with the help of stout poles which we found on the bank, it was an enjoyable crossing.

After emptying the water from our boots we put on Goretex socks over thin dry socks, before putting the boots back on. We found this to be a most satisfactory way of dealing with fords, it was great to be walking with warm, dry feet while our wet boots squelched with every step.

The trail followed an old woods road for a while, which made for easy walking, and passed through the Hermitage, an area of protected white pines some 130' tall. We then climbed 1100' alongside Gulf Hagas Brook before crossing it to reach the Carl Newhall lean-to, where we spent a sunny afternoon washing our smalls and the many socks we had used in fording rivers. Although we had seen several hikers on the trail, no-one else arrived so we had an early night.

Next day we traversed the White Cap Range, passing over Gulf Hagas Mountain (2,683'), West Peak (3,181'), Hay Mountain (3,244') and White Cap Mountain (3,644'). While making the first climb of the day we heard a helicopter flying around nearby, the noise was very intrusive in this wilderness area. It got closer and closer and eventually hovered over us when we stopped in a clearing. There was a crew member sitting at each of the open doors, obviously searching for something or somebody. We gave a "thumbs up" to tell them we were OK, and later learned that they were trying to find a hiker who was reported to have broken a leg.

The trail was in poor condition for the next few miles - very overgrown with lots of blowdowns across the path, one we had to crawl under on our knees and at another we had to take off our packs to get through. By the time we reached the summit of White Cap we were feeling quite tired, but as we started the descent there was the most wonderful view for a northbound hiker - Mount Katahdin some 40 miles away, but seeming close enough to reach out and touch. We sat on a rock for a break and just looked at the view that we had hiked more than 2,000 miles to see. It was a beautiful warm, sunny day and we could have stayed there for hours. Feeling revitalised, we started the 1,200' descent to Logan Brook lean-to where we arrived after hiking only 6.7 miles in 5.5 hours. We were joined for the night by Burton, a minister of the Moravian church, who was hiking the AT in sections over several years.

We followed Logan Brook down to the valley and forded the East Branch of the Pleasant River on rocks. After climbing Little Boardman Mountain (2,024') the remaining miles to Katahdin were reasonably flat as the trail meandered along streams and beside ponds, but it was rough and boggy in places. We made good time and saw many views of our objective which seemed to be drawing us towards it like a magnet. John was keen to get on and reach the end of the Trail, but Pam didn't want the adventure to end and would rather savour the last few days.

West Branch of the Pleasant River
Katahdin from White Cap

After passing Crawford Pond we followed Cooper Brook downstream to the shelter in a beautiful situation beside Cooper Brook Falls. We arrived at 12.15pm having hiked 11.6 miles, so we bathed in the deep pool at the foot of the falls and enjoyed the sunny afternoon at this picturesque spot. At about 2.30 we were joined by Ron "Jack Finn", the second northbound thru'-hiker of 1992, who stayed for the night.

It started raining in the early hours, but Ron was up and away by 5.30am. We were a bit more leisurely, but were still on the trail before 6.30 and the rain had stopped by 8 o'clock. It was a nice easy hike on a gentle downhill gradient to the western end of Lower Jo Mary Lake which we skirted for a while before climbing the ridge to reach Potaywadjo Spring lean-to where we had planned to stay the night. As we arrived there at 11.20am, we had a change of plan. After cooking some soup and rice for lunch we filled our water bottles at the enormous spring and then continued on our way to the next shelter.

The trail was rooty and boggy passing the upper end of Pemadumcook Lake, but then we hiked along Nahmakanta Stream for almost five miles upstream to the point where it flows out of Nahmakanta Lake. The trail was very pleasant as it followed the bank of this lovely salmon river. When we reached the lake we were surprised to find that the trail actually went into the water and we had to rock hop for about 200 yards before returning to solid ground. After climbing over a headland we found ourselves back down at the lake shore, then headed away from the water and arrived at Wadleigh Stream lean-to at 4.45pm. We had hiked 21.1 miles in 10 hours and 20 minutes. Three southbound hikers already had a fire going at the shelter and they were good company.

Next day was dry and mild as we set off at 6.10am to climb Nesuntabunt Mountain (1,560') for a good view of Mount Katahdin with it's head in the clouds. It was only 16 miles away as the crow flies, but we had 35 miles to hike on the Appalachian Trail to reach it. We stopped for a break on a sunny rock overlooking beautiful Crescent Pond, then continued down to Pollywog Stream which we followed downstream to cross it on a logging bridge. Then up picturesque Rainbow Stream with a 600' long cascade, to reach Rainbow Stream lean-to for our lunch break at 10.20am. This shelter is in another wonderful situation beside the stream; Maine just seemed to get more and more spectacular as we headed north.

After cooking soup and noodles we were on our way again within the hour, crossing the stream on a log bridge and continuing upstream past three ponds before reaching Rainbow Lake. Here was a wonderful view of Katahdin across the lake, the views were just getting better and better as we got closer.

We followed the edge of the lake for five miles on a hot, sunny afternoon and stopped to refill our water bottles at Rainbow Spring, right on the shore. At the end of the lake we started the easy climb up Rainbow Ledges, a lovely rocky ridge where we stopped in the sunshine and gorged ourselves on the wild blueberries, and admired yet another view of Mount Katahdin, before starting the long descent on a rough trail to Hurd Brook lean-to. We arrived at 5pm after hiking 19.1 miles and this was to be our last night in a shelter on the Appalachian Trail. We had mixed feelings as we went about our usual routine of chores - elation at being so close to our objective, but sadness at being almost at the end of the Trail which had become a way of life over the weeks and months of our adventure. A father and son were camping nearby on their way to Mount Katahdin and they came across for a chat in the evening, but we again had the shelter to ourselves.

It was an easy 3.4 miles to Abol Bridge where we arrived at 8am. There was another wonderful view of Mount Katahdin, but the short walk along the road was far from pleasant with huge logging trucks loaded with timber roaring past sending up choking clouds of dust. We went to the store, the first since Monson, to buy our last supply of groceries and to treat ourselves to all sorts of treats for the final two days. We had come through the "100-mile wilderness" in seven days and had seen more hikers than on many other stretches of the Trail. We had been very lucky with the weather and had really enjoyed this beautiful remote area of forests and lakes.

It was a beautiful warm, sunny morning and we enjoyed the pleasant walk along the Penobscot River, but civilization was nearby as we could hear traffic on the main road across the river. We stopped to watch a group of canoeists in the rapids at the point where Nesowadnehunk Stream flows into the Penobscot River, before we turned north to follow the stream as far as Daicey Pond campsite. We scrambled upstream over rocky ledges with lovely views of the stream tumbling over rocks and waterfalls on it's way down to join the river. We reached Daicey Pond campsite at 11.45am and checked in with a very friendly ranger to register and enter Baxter State Park. The view of Katahdin across Daicey Pond was quite stunning as we sat on the little jetty soaking our feet and eating lunch. The sky was blue and the sun was shining, and we tried to imagine how we would feel in 24 hours time when we should be sitting up there on top of Baxter Peak at the end of the Appalachian Trail.

We had planned to stay the night at Daicey Pond campsite, but as it was early, we asked the ranger if he would radio ahead to see if there would be room for us to camp at Katahdin Stream campground. We were told that there was space available in the bunkhouse so we set off on the two mile hike to the very foot of Mount Katahdin. After following the shore of Daicey Pond we had to cross the outlet streams of two other ponds, both quite tricky and requiring the use of poles for balance. While we were wandering along the trail, lost in our thoughts, we were brought to our senses by a voice exclaiming "The Olde Yorkies"! It was "Slo Jo", whom we had previously met at Andover and Monson. She had driven to Baxter State Park and was hiking south from Katahdin back to Monson with a friend. They proceeded to tell us just how difficult they had found the climb and descent of Mount Katahdin - it had taken them 5 hours in each direction - and they were so exhausted afterwards they had needed to rest for two days before starting to hike south. We felt confident that we would not find it that difficult as we had negotiated all the other mountains on the Trail, many with a similar height gain, without too much trouble. But next day we were to remember their warning.......... !

When we arrived at Katahdin Stream we met "Jack Finn" who had climbed Katahdin that morning and had just returned to the campsite, becoming the second thru'-hiker of 1992. He told us that "Fairhope" had finished his hike two days earlier.

At the bunkhouse we noticed that there was a sleeping bag spread out on one of the bunks so we expected company for the night. Our companion arrived back from a short stroll later. She was Karen, a Methodist pastor from Georgia, whose husband had died recently and she felt that she had received a divine message linking Georgia with Maine and compelling her to hike between those two states. So she had bought the necessary equipment and, with no previous hiking experience, was about to set off on a thru'-hike of the Appalachian Trail from north to south. She asked us a lot of questions, and we helped her as much as possible, but we were rather concerned for her safety. However, she was determined to do her best, and we wished her luck on her mission. Although we gave her our address we haven't heard how she fared.

Next morning we awoke at 5am to find that it was raining, so we stayed in bed for another hour. The weather didn't look very promising but the forecast on the radio said that it would clear in the afternoon. By 8 o'clock the cloud had started to lift so we set off to climb the final 5.2 miles of the Appalachian Trail, with lightweight packs as we would be returning to the campground. We made good time to treeline, but then the going became very tough with huge steep boulders, some with iron hand/foot grips to make the climb possible. At times we had to take off our packs to haul ourselves up through narrow cracks between rocks.

When we got to within 1.5 miles of the summit the wind got up and the cloud rolled in all around us. We were still negotiating the steep, rocky climb and didn't know how much further it would continue, it was very frightening and we remembered "Slo Jo's" warning. We were worried that the weather would deteriorate further so, after some hugs and tears, we reluctantly decided to go down rather than risk the unknown in bad weather conditions. We were very upset that we were about to admit defeat after coming so far. When we had descended about ten yards, John sat down on a rock to reconsider - we had a quick "huggle" and decided to continue to the top. It was like in a dream, as soon as we started climbing again the clouds began to lift and the sun came out.

We were soon at the end of the rocky section and on the Tableland, a large plateau which we crossed before the final rocky slope to the summit. The sun was shining and we could see for miles across the beautiful lakes and forests of Maine. At noon on 21st July 1992 we were the only people on Baxter Peak (5,267') of Mount Katahdin, so we had to take celebratory photographs using the self-timer and with the camera balanced rather precariously on a rock!

We passed several other hikers coming up as we returned to the campground. We slowly walked back across the Tableland and sat on a rock to eat our lunch, enjoying the wonderful views in the now perfect visibility. The steep descent down the boulders was not frightening now that we could see around us and we managed to lower ourselves and our packs down the difficult sections without any trouble. We could now appreciate the lovely walk down through the trees and past the waterfalls, which we had ignored on the way up in our eagerness to reach the summit. We arrived back at the campground at 4.05pm, it had

Climbing Hunt Spur, Mt Katahdin
End of the Trail

taken us 7 hours and 55 minutes to hike the 10.4 miles up and down Katahdin. It was definitely the most difficult mountain we had to negotiate on the whole Trail, but a fitting end to a great hike.

Our life's big adventure was over, we had hiked 2,146 miles through 14 states to complete the Appalachian Trail. It was with very mixed feelings that we repacked our rucksacks for the last time and walked to the road to thumb a lift out of the Park. Within five minutes we were sitting in the back of a pickup truck, bouncing along the dirt road to the town of Millinocket, with Mount Katahdin receding rapidly from view. That mountain had been our goal since we first began to plan our hike more than four years ago and now it was behind us. We had first seen Katahdin from 100 miles away more than two weeks ago, and had watched it grow ever larger in our sights as we slowly approached along the Trail. It was with lumps in our throats that we saw it disappear as we were whisked back into civilization. Our wonderful adventure was behind us, but we are left with so many memories of the beautiful places we have seen, the wild animals that have accepted us in their world and of the wonderful people we met both on and off the Trail.

People more clever than us have calculated that in hiking the Appalachian Trail you walk five million steps, climb and descend 88.3 miles (the equivalent of more than 16 Mount Everests from sea level to summit!) and secrete more than 100 gallons of sweat. Be this as it may, we simply shouldered our packs, put one foot in front of the other and followed the white blazes from Georgia to Maine.

Chapter 9

EQUIPMENT REPORT

We were very pleased with the performance of our kit and, with very few exceptions, would use the same again. The following is a list of the equipment we took on the Trail with comments which may be of use to future hikers.

Rucksacks.

In 1990 we both used Berghaus Cyclops II Scorpion rucksacks, John's had 100 litre capacity and Pam's 90 litres. These took all our gear, but John had trouble with the frame wearing through the fabric at the base. He had this repaired by a cobbler en route and, on our return, it was replaced with an Atlas by Berghaus as the Scorpion had been discontinued. We also used Berghaus rucksack covers to protect the packs. Not only did they keep them dry, but also prevented the packs becoming dirty when we dropped them on the ground to sit on them for a rest. Unfortunately these are no longer available and we have been unable to find any of such good quality.

In 1992 John used his Berghaus Atlas and found it very comfortable and commodious, in fact he did not take the side pockets and it was still plenty big enough. Pam tried a Vaude Terkum, with adjustable harness which helped to retain a good fit as she lost weight. There was some discomfort, however, as the padding on the hip-belt tended to ride up under heavy load allowing the rigid plastic belt to press into the hips. Both these packs gave good service, with no failures.

Tent.

In 1990 we took a Phoenix Phunnel tent (8 lbs) which was very roomy for the two of us, but as we only used it on five occasions we decided to change to the Pheonix Phreebooter (5.5lbs) for the 1992 trip. This was a good decision as we only used it three times on that hike. We did find that in the heat of summer we needed more ventilation than that provided by the single netting door and, for future hikers, would recommend a tent with as much netting as possible. Most American tents pitch inner first, giving the option of sleeping without the flysheet in hot weather. This would be preferable and, with lots of netting panels, it can be used as a mosquito-net - even inside shelters if they are not too crowded. A free-standing tent would also be preferred as many campsites have wooden tent platforms, making it rather difficult (but not impossible) to secure guys and pegs (take some small cuphooks!). We used our Vango emergency survival-bag (double size) under the tent to protect the groundsheet from damage by stones,etc.

Sleeping-bags.

We both used Mountain Equipment Lightline down sleeping-bags, and North Cape silk liners which protected the bags from perspiration and prevented them from becoming too smelly during prolonged use. These also gave additional warmth in cold weather and were used on their own in hot weather (lying on top of our down bags). We found our Therm-a-Rest ¾-length ultralight mattresses to be very comfortable. To prevent them sliding apart we joined them together with a "Couple Kit" and also sprayed them with "Slip-Fix" to prevent the sleeping-bags slipping off the mattresses. In shelters, all this went on top of our Vango survival-bag which prevented our bedding from becoming soiled on the wooden floors.

Cooking Kit.

Our MSR Whisperlite Internationale stove gave good service on both trips, being very lightweight and efficient. We found Coleman fuel was easy to obtain, often "by the pint" at stores along the Trail and we never had to use any other type of fuel. We did notice that butane gas cartridges were very difficult to find, usually only available from camping stores in towns, so would not recommend a stove using this type of fuel for use on the AT. Our stove fitted inside the smallest of the Bulldog pans (we only took the 2 smaller ones of the 3-pan set). These also gave good service both on the stove and on campfires, and we found the bucket-type handles very useful for carrying water from streams, but we also had a gripper handle for pouring. We each had a plastic plate and mug, a Swiss Army knife, dessertspoon and teaspoon (we used the dessertspoon for anything we would normally eat with a fork) and a wooden spoon for stirring the pots.

Water Treatment.

ATC strongly recommend treating all water for drinking. We found the most convenient form of treatment to be a filter pump, as boiling took too long and we felt that using iodine for such a long period would be inadvisable. We started out with a Filopur filter as it was very lightweight, but the filters could not cope with the silty water and rapidly blocked and required replacement. We then bought a Katadyn pocket filter which was very effective and reliable, but it is quite heavy and the pumping action is awkward. This gave good service for the rest of the 1990 trip, but we then discovered the MSR Waterworks filter, which is lighter in weight than the Katadyn and has a more natural pumping action. An additional bonus is that it screws onto the Nalgene water bottles and the MSR waterbag. So we took this with us in 1992. Unfortunately we found that it required a lot of field maintenance as filters became blocked, and it was difficult to judge which of the four filters had failed. This meant carrying several replacement filters in our kit. So we cannot really recommend any of the pumps we have tried (although the Katadyn was the most reliable). From studying the equipment of other hikers on the Trail we feel that the First Need may be the best buy as it is cheap, simple and didn't appear to give any trouble.

We used a 7-litre Liquipak waterbag for carrying water from the stream or spring to the campsite/shelter and later added a MSR Dromedary 4-litre bag (we used one for "raw" water and one for purified water). This may seem excessive, but we found we needed 10 litres of water at each nightstop for drinking, cooking, washing and washing-up. As many water sources were some way down the ridge it was useful to be able to collect enough water in one visit. We each carried a 1-litre Nalgene water bottle for drinking water on the trail.

First Aid Kit.

Our basic kit was the Gregson Pack with the addition of Diocare, moleskin and corn plasters. Fortunately we rarely had to use our medical kit. However, we did make good use of the following:- sunblock cream, insect repellent (we found "Off" to be most effective), hydrocortisone cream (to stop itching caused by insect bites or poison-ivy), Vaseline and lip salve.

Boots.

John used Brasher Hillmasters and found he needed two pairs for the 1100 miles in 1990 and two pairs for 1050 miles in 1992, but he estimates that to hike the entire 2146 miles in one go would require 2 or 3 pairs as there was still plenty of life left in the second pair after each hike. Pam preferred to use the slightly heavier Zamberlan Treklites and used one pair on each hike, but the first pair would probably have lasted for an entire "thru-hike". We both used Sorbothane footbeds in our boots, and wore Goretex gaiters in all but the hottest weather.

Clothing.

As we were hiking through three seasons we used the layer system of clothing so that we could adjust to the conditions, yet carry the minimum amount. We used wicking underwear (Helly Hansen and Patagonia), various long and short sleeved wicking vests and pile or fleece jackets. John wore Rohan bags and Pam used Ultimate polycotton trousers - over longjohns in cold weather. In summer we both wore Rohan shorts. For visits to town we kept a set of polycotton trousers and Rohan safari shirt "for best", and were often complimented on how smart we looked! We took trainers to wear in town and around the shelter at night. We each had 3 pairs of thick hiking socks and 3 pairs of Helly Hansen inner socks. The inners lasted the whole trip, but we had to replace the thick socks as they wore out en route. We also bought cheap T-shirts as required.

In 1990 we wore Berghaus Lightning Goretex jackets in the cool weather at the start of the hike and replaced them with the lightweight Montbell Stormcruiser Goretex jackets as the weather warmed up (we used the Montbell Stormcruiser rainpants throughout). In 1992 we used Nikwax Paramo jackets as warm, breathable waterproofs and were delighted with them. We again used the lightweight Montbells in the summer.

Our other items of clothing were wool or pile hats, sun hats, polypropylene gloves, Goretex mitts and Goretex socks. And Pam used a Leki Lightwalk walking stick.

Camera.

In 1990 we used a Konica Z-up 80 camera which was lightweight and seemed ideal as it was a point and shoot with zoom facility. It should have been foolproof, but unfortunately the auto-focus mechanism did not work too well, a problem we didn't discover until we came off the Trail and viewed our 15 films. (We had used it successfully prior to our AT hike, but the problem developed gradually while on the Trail). So, having learned from our experience, we bought a Minolta 5000i with a zoom lens, which is also point and shoot, but as it is a SLR camera we could see that the shot was in focus before pressing the button. We had no problems with this on our 1992 hike. On both occasions we carried the cameras on a waist belt in cases made by Camera Care Systems of Bristol. These protected the cameras from knocks and scrapes on rocks and from the weather. They were only put away inside rucksacks in really heavy rain (when we wouldn't be using them anyway) and when fording rivers.

Most of the time we used Fujichrome 100 film, which we bought whenever in a town. In America you buy the mailing envelope for slide processing as a separate item. These are usually only available from photographic shops, so when we found some we would buy several. This meant that we could mail the film away for processing from the first mailbox we saw, rather than having to carry it to the next town. We had the processed slides sent to our friend Chuck, so he could check that the camera was working OK! The US Mail managed to lose one of our films in 1990, but we can see no alternative apart from keeping the spools with you which would risk loss or damage from heat or moisture.

In 1992 we also carried a Halina Panorama camera (weight 3oz), which produced some acceptable panoramic snapshots from mountain tops in bright weather conditions despite being a very basic plastic box camera. In this we used Fujicolour 200 film.

Radio.

We bought a very small Sony Walkman radio (with earphones, but no cassette player) in Washington before travelling to Georgia. This was used to listen to weather forecasts and proved very useful in warning us of approaching belts of bad weather. However we did find it difficult to locate the correct time and station, and it was just "pot luck" if we happened to find what we were looking for amongst all the pop music and adverts. If there was a young hiker with us in the shelter we overcame the problem by handing him the radio. He would be happy to sit listening to the music and then relayed the weather forecast to us when it came on!

When we were on the Trail in Virginia in 1992 we noticed that another hiker was listening to very detailed weather forecasts whenever he switched on his radio. We discovered that he was using a Weather Radio - one made solely for receiving broadcasts from a 24 hour weather service. We purchased one of these sets for $17 from Radio Shack in the next town we visited and found it gave excellent service. (It is of no use when you return to Britain though, so we gave it to a friend who had been very helpful to us in America).

Miscellaneous Items.

Washing/shaving kit, towel, handkerchiefs, J-cloths, pan-scourer, washing-up liquid (in small plastic bottle), 2 fuel bottles, stuff sac for food, paracord, a few plastic clothes pegs, earplugs, torch, whistle, compass, films, toilet paper and trowel, lighter and matches, airmail notepad and pen, guidebooks/maps, passports and credit cards.

Chapter 10

FOOD

There are two methods commonly used for obtaining food along the Trail. Many American hikers buy dehydrated food in bulk before the hike, repackage it in meal-size bags and then leave it for a friend or relation to mail ahead to post offices along the way. This method would be difficult for a hiker from Britain to organise, so we just mention it in passing.

The method we used was to simply buy food as we went along. This obviously involved coming off the Trail at frequent intervals, but visiting small towns and villages was one of the many pleasures of the hike. The selection of suitable food was limited at small country stores, although most are used to the requirements of hikers so there was always some sort of rice or pasta available. And many make a real effort by stocking Coleman fuel and small items of hiking gear such as socks and moleskin! In larger towns the supermarkets were full of convenience foods which were ideal for our needs.

The following are some of the foods which were quick and easy to cook and readily available in stores along the way (we repackaged most items into meal-sized portions in ziplock bags):-

Breakfast.
Instant oats, packaged in individual sachets in various flavours
Cereal, a vast variety of muesli, etc
Granola bars, Poptarts and Nutrigrain bars
Dried milk - Carnation seemed to mix best without lumps
Sugar, in small plastic jar and refilled at diners, etc (ask first!)
Tang - powdered orange juice

Lunch.
>Bread - pumpernickel was firm and didn't break up
English muffins
Margarine, various makes available in squeeze bottles
Cheese (Cracker Barrel seemed to keep well)
Peanut butter, full of calories if you can stomach it!

Dinner.
>Cup-a-soups
Minute rice, soak for 4 mins. in boiling water (no cooking)
Liptons noodles/ rice with sauce (many flavours)
Ramen noodles
Instant potato
Macaroni cheese
Small tins of tuna, chicken, etc to add to pasta, rice, potatoes
Gravy mix
Textured soya protein, available from health food stores
Salt, pepper, herbs, spices (carry in emptied film canisters)
Dried onions, peppers, mushrooms, mixed vegetables

Drinks.
>Tea bags (we preferred Red Rose when we could find them)
Coffee bags or instant coffee
Drinking Chocolate sachets - Swiss Miss were very good
Dried milk powder (preferably Carnation)
Gatorade (isotonic drink powder, available in sachets)
Kool Aid (fruit flavoured drink powder)
Jello - fruit flavoured gelatin powder (for making jelly), but if well diluted with hot water it makes a refreshing hot drink (lime or lemon were the most refreshing)

Snacks.
- Gorp ("good old raisins and peanuts"!)
- Dried fruit (apples, prunes, apricots, etc)
- Mars bars, etc
- M & Ms
- Granola bars

And in case that lot doesn't give enough nutrition - multivitamins and minerals.

Chapter 11

FURTHER INFORMATION FOR BRITISH HIKERS

U.S. Visas.

British hikers will need to get a U.S. Non-Immigrant Visa - this entitles you to stay in America for up to six months. (Do not rely on the visa waiver you can obtain on the inbound flight to America - these are only valid for 90 days). You can get a Visa application (Form 156) from The U.S. Embassy, Visa Branch, 5 Upper Grosvenor Street, London, W1A 2JB.

Money.

We found that the best way to organise our finances was to use credit cards to pay for lodging, bus or rail tickets, mail order of equipment, guide books, etc and to get cash advances from banks. We were surprised to find that most supermarkets do NOT take credit cards for food so we always carried some cash or travellers cheques with us. (You obviously have to have arranged for somebody at home to settle the credit card bills each month!)

Travel Insurance.

We recommend you get a good insurance policy, it's not worth cutting costs on this - medical expenses are very high in America - and with insurance you get what you pay for.

FURTHER INFORMATION ON THE APPALACHIAN TRAIL MAY BE OBTAINED FROM:-

Appalachian Trail Conference
PO BOX 807
Harpers Ferry
West Virginia 25425-0807
U.S.A.

Index

Abol Bridge 131
Addis Gap shelter 33
Albert Mountain 35
AMC 94, 108, 110
Andover 114, 115, 117, 122, 125, 132
Appalachian Mountain Club 87, 94, 107
Apple Valley Inn 80, 81
ATC 3, 8-11, 15, 19, 22, 46, 54, 59, 64, 71, 74, 122, 139
Atkins 49
Atwell Hilton 104, 106
AYH 24, 63
Bake Oven Knob shelter 29
Bascom Lodge 94
Baxter State Park 132
Bear Mountain Inn 83
Bearfence Mountain Hut 59
Bears Den Youth Hostel 63
Bemis Mountain lean-to 115
Benton MacKaye 9, 97
Big Branch shelter 99
Big Meadows Lodge 59
Big Spring shelter 35
Bigelow shelter 97
Birch Spring shelter 40
Blackburn Trail Centre 64
Blackrock Hut 56
Blacksburg 53
Blue Mountain Eagle Climbing Club hostel 26
Blue Mountain shelter 33
Blue Ridge Parkway 7, 68, 72

Bobblets Gap shelter	72
Brink Road shelter	78
Brown Mountain Creek shelter	74
Cable Gap shelter	38
Calf Mountain shelter	56
Caratunk	122, 123
Carl Newhall lean-to	127
Carter Notch Hut	111
Catawba	55, 67, 69, 55
Chairback Gap lean-to	126
Charlie's Bunion	42
Chatfield shelter	49
Chattahoochee National Forest	31
Cherry Gap shelter	44
Chesapeake & Ohio Canal	21
Cheshire	94
Chestnut Knob shelter	51
Clarendon shelter	100
Cloudland shelter	103
Cloverdale	71
Cold Spring shelter	36
Connecticut	9, 42, 72, 86-88, 93, 95, 104
Cooper Brook Falls	130
Cooper Lodge	100
Cornelius Creek shelter	73
Cow Camp Gap shelter	74
Crampton Gap shelter	21
Crawford Notch	110
Cumberland Valley	25, 76
Dahlonega	30
Daicey Pond	16, 132
Dalton	94
Damascus	47, 48
Dartmouth Outing Club	104

Data Book	11
Davenport Gap shelter	42
Deep Gap shelter	49
Delaware Water Gap	30, 67, 76
Dick's Dome shelter	62
Doc's Knob shelter	52
Double Spring Gap shelter	41
Dragon's Tooth	69
Duncannon	25, 76
Eagles Nest shelter	27
Eliza Brook shelter	107
Elizabethton	47
Erwin	44
Fahnestock State Park	84
Fontana	38, 39
Franconia Notch	107, 108
Front Royal	61
Frye Notch lean-to	114
Full Goose lean-to	113
Fullhardt Knob shelter	71
Gainesville	30
Galehead Hut	108
Gathland State Park	21
Gentian Pond shelter	112
George Washington National Forest	48
Georgia	1, 6, 7, 11, 15, 29-32, 62, 76, 79, 125, 133, 136, 143
Glen Brook shelter	90
Gorham	104, 111
Governor Clement shelter	100
Grafton Notch lean-to	114
Gravel Springs Hut	60
Graymoor Monastery	83
Green Mountains	95, 96, 101
Greenleaf Hut	108

Groundhog Creek shelter	42
Hall Mountain lean-to	115
Hampton	47
Hanover	104, 111
Happy Hill Cabin	103
Harpers Creek shelter	75
Harpers Ferry	8, 10, 15, 21, 27, 57, 59, 62, 64, 65, 148
Harrisburg	25, 76
Hawk Mountain shelter	31, 37
Helveys Mill shelter	51
Hightop Hut	58
Hoosic River	94, 95
Hot Springs	43, 47
Housatonic River	87, 89, 90
Hudson River	83
Hurd Brook lean-to	131
Hurricane Hugo	49
Icewater Spring	41
Imp shelter	111
James River	73
Jeffers Brook shelter	106
Jefferson National Forest	48
Jenny Knob shelter	52
Jim and Molly Denton shelter	62
Joe's Hole lean-to	124
Katahdin	6, 11, 16, 27, 67, 76, 79, 105, 112, 116, 119, 128-136
Kennebec River	122
Keys Gap shelter	65
Kid Gore shelter	96
Killington Peak	100
Kinsman Notch	107
Knot Maul Branch shelter	50, 51
Konnarock Crew	54
Lake of the Clouds Hut	110

Lambert's Meadow shelter	69
Laurel Creek	49
Laurel Falls	47
Laurel Fork Gorge	47
Lehigh Gap	29
Lemon Squeezer	82
Lewis Mountain campground	58
Little Rock Pond shelter	99
Loft Mountain campground	57
Logan Brook lean-to	128
Lonesome Lake Hut	107
Long Pond Stream lean-to	126
Long Trail	96, 101
Lost Pond shelter	99
Low Gap shelter	33
Mad Tom shelter	98
Mahoosuc Notch	112, 113
Maine	1, 6, 7, 11, 67, 76, 101, 112, 113, 115-117, 119, 121, 122, 125, 131, 133, 134, 136
Maine Junction	101
Manassas Gap shelter	62
Manchester	97
Manhattan	82
Maryland	15, 21, 23, 31
Mashipacong shelter	79
Matts Creek shelter	73
Maupin Field shelter	75
Max Patch	43
McAfee Knob	69
Melville Neuheim shelter	96
Minerva Hinchey shelter	100
Monson	125, 126, 131, 132
Moreland Gap shelter	46
Morgan Stewart shelter	85

Mount Greylock	90, 94, 96
Mount Kinsman	107
Mount Moosilauke	107
Mount Rogers	49
Mount Washington	110
Mount Willcox North shelter	92
Moxie Bald Mountain Pond	124
Muskrat Creek shelter	34
Myron Avery	9, 120
Myron Avery lean-to	120
Nantahala National Forest	34
Nantahala Outdoor Center	37
Nantahala River	37
Neel's Gap	32
New Hampshire	95, 101, 104, 112, 115, 120
New Jersey	30, 76, 78-80, 86, 92
New York	6, 20, 26, 76, 79, 81, 83, 85-87
Newfound Gap	7, 41
Niday shelter	55
Nolichucky River	44
North Carolina	7, 34, 39, 43, 44, 75
Norwich	103
October Mountain shelter	93
Palmerton	29, 30
Panorama	60
Paul Wolfe Memorial shelter	67
Peaks of Otter	72, 73
Pearisburg	53
Pennsylvania	6, 15, 21, 23-26, 29-32, 51, 65, 67, 76-78
Penobscot River	132
Peru Peak shelter	99
Peters Mountain shelter	26
Pico Camp	101
Pierce Pond lean-to	121

Pine Grove Furnace State Park	24
Pine Swamp Branch shelter	53
Pine Swamp Brook shelter	88
Pinefield Hut	57
Pinkham Notch	110
Pinnacle	28
Pleasant Pond lean-to	123
Plumorchard Gap shelter	33
Poplar Ridge lean-to	119
Port Clinton	27
Potaywadjo Spring lean-to	130
Potomac River	21
Presidential Range	110, 112
Punchbowl shelter	73
Raccoon Branch shelter	49
Rainbow Springs campground	36
Rainbow Stream lean-to	131
Ralph's Peak Hikers Cabin	84
Rangeley	117
Rausch Gap shelter	26
Riga shelter	90
Roan High Knob shelter	45
Roanoke	68, 69, 71
Roaring Fork shelter	43
Rock Spring Hut	59
Rockfish Gap	56, 67
Rod Hollow shelter	63
Rusty's	68, 69, 75
Rutherford shelter	79
Sabbath Pond lean-to	117
Saddleback	117
Sages Ravine	90
Salisbury	90
Sassafras Gap shelter	37

Saunders shelter 48
Seeley-Woodworth shelter 75
Seth Warner shelter 95
Shenandoah National Park 48, 56, 57, 61, 64
Shenandoah River 65
Shenandoah Valley 60, 64
Sherburne Pass 100
Skyland 60
Skyline Drive 57, 60, 57
Smokies 7, 38, 39, 41-43, 56, 89
Smoky Mountains 7, 38-40, 42
Spaulding Mountain lean-to 119
Speck Pond lean-to 114
Spence Field shelter 40
Springer Mountain 11, 15, 20, 27, 30, 31, 37, 44, 57, 76
St. John's Ledges 88
Stecoah Gap 38
Stewart Hollow Brook shelter 88
Stony Brook shelter 102
Story Spring shelter 97
Stratton 120
Stratton Mountain 97
Stratton Pond 97
Sugarloaf 117, 119, 120
Susquehanna River 76
Swatara Gap 26
Tennessee 7, 34, 39, 44, 47
The Priest 75
Thru-Hiker's Handbook 11, 12
Thunder Hill shelter 73
Tom Floyd Wayside shelter 61
Tom Leonard shelter 92
Trail Magic 37, 80
Trout Creek 55, 69

Tye River	75
Tyringham	92
Unionville	79, 80
Upper Goose Pond	93
Virginia	6, 8, 10, 24, 47-49, 53, 64, 65, 67-69, 75, 76, 143, 148
Wadleigh Stream lean-to	130
Wapiti shelter	52
War Spur Branch shelter	54
Wawayanda shelter	81
Webatuck shelter	86
West Carry Pond	121
West Virginia	8, 10, 48, 53, 64, 65, 148
White Mountains	104, 107, 109, 110, 120
William Brien Memorial shelter	82
Wilson Creek Shelter	72
Wintturi shelter	102
Zealand Falls Hut	108